AN INTRODUCTORY TEACHING COURSE ON SPIRITUAL

Contents

Introduction to the course	page 2
Summary of the Course	page 3
'If you are a Minister read this...'	page 4

Course Leader's Guide — page 5

Leaders' Assessment Sheet	page 6
Week 1: 'The God who gives gifts'. Central gathering with initial talk, led by the Minister.	page 7
Group Members' Sheet	page 10
Handout Notes for Keynote Talk	page 11
Outline of Minister's Keynote Talk for Week 1: 'The God who gives gifts'	page 13
Week 2: 'All right with God' - in housegroups.	page 17
Group Members' Sheet	page 19
Week 3: 'For what we are about to receive' - in housegroups.	page 21
Group Members' Sheet	page 23

Meeting of housegroup leaders and minister

Week 4: 'Gifts from God'. Central gathering, led by the Minister.	page 25
Act of Commitment (optional)	page 27
Week 5: 'Equipping the Saints' - in housegroups.	page 29
Group Members' Sheet	page 31
Individual Assessment Sheet	page 33
Week 6: 'Moving On'. Central gathering, led by the Minister.	page 35

Resource Sections — page 37

1 Questions and Answers	page 38
2 Ministry in the Local Church by Graham Cray	page 39
3 Leadership in the Local Church by Graham Cray	page 49
4 Spiritual gifts and personal ministry by Graham Cray	page 57
5 Gifts of the Spirit in the Local Church	page 59
6 Going on from here	page 63

INTRODUCTION TO THE COURSE

Welcome to 'Tools for the Job', a local church project on spiritual gifts. We trust that your church will experience genuine growth as a result of being involved in this course. Spiritual gifts are God's inheritance for all his people, enabling them together to serve him in the church and in the world. There is plenty of material available here and not all of it will be relevant to everyone. Begin by looking at those sections which particularly apply to your situation.

The project had its beginnings some three years ago under the leadership of Derek Little. In February 1988 there was a pilot day in Cambridge when Graham Cray (Vicar of St. Michael-le-Belfry, York) delivered a keynote address. We are greatly indebted to Graham for his enthusiasm for the project and for his willingness to allow us to use his 'St Michael-le-Belfrey' papers relating to spiritual gifts.

Following the pilot teaching day, a six-week course was field tested in a number of churches in the East of England. We are most grateful to these churches; their comments have resulted in further revision. The project before you, therefore, has undergone considerable revision and field-testing and we commend it to you with confidence.

The Project Team

RECOMMENDED REFERENCE BOOK

Your Spiritual Gifts Can Help Your Church Grow C Peter Wagner *(MARC) £4.50*
- **Available from CPAS Sales** Falcon Court
  32 Fleet Street London EC4Y 1DB
  Tel: 01-353 0751

SUMMARY OF THE COURSE

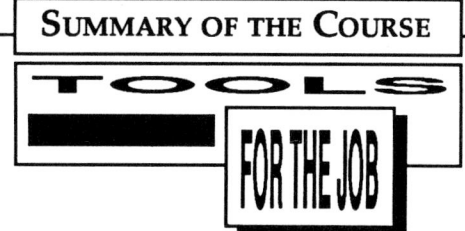

Week 1 'The God who gives gifts'. Central gathering with initial talk, led by the Minister.

Week 2 'All right with God' - in housegroups.

Week 3 'For what we are about to receive' - in housegroups.

Meeting of housegroup leaders and minister.

Week 4 'Gifts from God'. Central gathering, led by the Minister.

Week 5 'Equipping the Saints' - in housegroups.

Week 6 'Moving On'. Central gathering, led by the Minister.

● If you are a MINISTER you will want to have an overview of the whole project. We recommend that you begin by reading 'If you are a Minister read this...' (page 4) and then the COURSE LEADER'S GUIDE (page 5 onwards) and GOING ON FROM HERE (page 63).

● If you are a HOUSEGROUP LEADER look particularly at:

COURSE LEADER'S GUIDE	page 5 onwards
Leader's Assessment Sheet	page 6
Individual Assessment Sheet	page 33

For more detailed reading look at

RESOURCE SECTIONS

1. Questions and Answers	page 38
2. Ministry in the Local Church	page 39
3. Leadership In the Local Church	page 49
4. Spiritual Gifts and Personal Ministry	page 57
5. Gifts of the Spirit in the Local Church	page 59

● If you are a MEMBER of your church then you will only be required to use the Group Members' Sheets and the Individual Assessment Sheet. We leave it up to you to decide whether you want to read the more detailed sections of the course.

COPYRIGHT INFORMATION

(P) PERMISSION is given to photocopy sufficient Group Members' Sheets to meet the requirements of a single group. (see inside front cover)

IF YOU ARE A MINISTER READ THIS...

'Tools for the Job' is designed to help churches move forward in their understanding and use of spiritual gifts. We trust that you will find the material helpful and instructive for your own situation. It is likely that you will want to adapt what is set out here to ensure the course meets the needs of your church.

Experience has shown that the course will run more smoothly if group leaders are able to work through the material together in advance. Taking them out of their groups for a few weeks to do the course with them is well worthwhile.

We highly recommend as a very useful resource book: (See page 2 for details)
    Your Spiritual Gifts Can Help Your Church Grow
    C Peter Wagner *(MARC)* **£4.50**

The course has a specific aim with definite spiritual objectives. The method of learning is directive, and fairly structured, and locked into a specific programme. This is deliberate policy and may prove necessary if your church is to move forward in unity. Just as a Parish Mission provides a focus for everyone to become involved in evangelism, so a project like this can be the focus of renewal.

THE MINISTER'S ROLE

The Minister's role is crucial. You should be committed to the aims of the course and be prepared to give a lead. This is especially important at two points:

1.   When giving the initial talk, it is vital that you spell out clearly the purpose of the course and what you are expecting the church to gain from it. Outline the way you see the course being relevant to your own situation and add suitable discussion questions to bring this out. Stress also how important it is that everyone attends each session - otherwise people may get an unbalanced view of spiritual gifts.

2.   Between sessions 3 and 4 a meeting with your group leaders and other church leaders is highly recommended. This will help to clarify the priorities of the course and will provide an opportunity to see if God is saying new things through the insights of the housegroups.

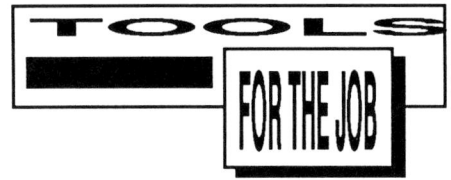

COURSE LEADER'S GUIDE
If you are a housegroup leader read this section

• WEEK 1	THE GOD WHO GIVES GIFTS
• WEEK 2	ALL RIGHT WITH GOD
• WEEK 3	FOR WHAT WE ARE ABOUT TO RECEIVE
• WEEK 4	GIFTS FROM GOD
• WEEK 5	EQUIPPING THE SAINTS
• WEEK 6	MOVING ON

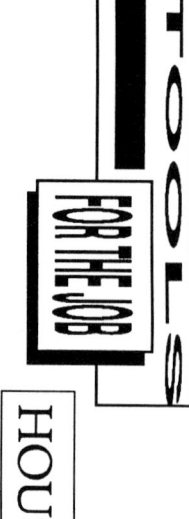

HOUSEGROUP LEADERS' ASSESSMENT SHEET

This is a weekly checklist to help you evaluate the group's work. It will also help you as you pray for the group and make it easier to report back to your leaders' meeting.

The Group

Week No

How many came?

Who was away and do I know why?

THE GROUP SESSION
Did we achieve the aim?
If not, why not?

Did the prayer and worship time achieve what I hoped for?
If not, why not?

GENERAL
Things I would do differently.

Was the Worksheet helpful in directing the group forward?

Would you have liked further information on any aspect?

Were there are encouragements or discouragements?

Was there anything which
a) could have been left out?
b) should have been included?

EXTRA NOTES

Ⓟ This sheet may be photocopied for local use   © Copyright CPAS 1990

COURSE LEADER'S GUIDE

WEEK 1

"THE GOD WHO GIVES GIFTS"

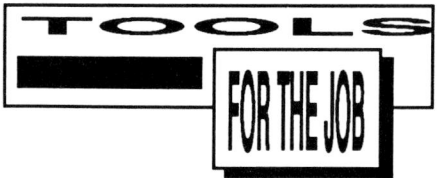

WEEK 1 "THE GOD WHO GIVES GIFTS"

This will be a central gathering (in a hall or church) and it is vital that everyone attends this first meeting. Housegroups will meet individually for part of the evening. Such an arrangement preserves group identity and discourages people from taking a 'night off'.

OVERALL AIM

To introduce the subject, clear away intellectual and spiritual debris and help people to see what needs to be done a) in their own life, and b) in the life of their church.

NEEDED FOR THIS SESSION

1   Photocopies of the Group Members Sheet - Week 1 and a supply of pens/pencils. Not everyone will have brought one.

2   An overhead projector, pens and blank slides for writing down answers.

3   Bibles. Using a church Bible ensures that everyone has the same translation.

4   Photocopies of Hand-out for Keynote Talk p 11 & 12 (optional).

5   Material to help the Minister to prepare the talk:
    - Outline of Minister's Keynote Talk for week 1   page 13
    - Resource Sections   page 37

OUTLINE OF THE SESSION

1   Welcome and a brief time of worship, including singing/reading/prayer (20 minutes)
2   Keynote talk, with activity (30 minutes)
3   Tasks in housegroups (25 minutes)
4   Teaching session together (25 minutes)

Although you must decide on your own timings, we strongly recommend that items 3 and 4 are not cut down. The schedule above lasts 1 hour 40 minutes.

Keynote talk: an outline is provided but clearly the Minister will need to tailor the talk to meet the needs of his own church. Choose those things which are new to the congregation whilst briefly reinforcing things which are familiar.

TASKS IN HOUSEGROUPS

At the end of the talk, get into housegroups around the church/hall. Some thought needs to be given to those who are not regular members of housegroups and it would be helpful to know in advance how many will be attending. They can either be incorporated into existing groups or form their own small group(s), provided someone suitable is available to act as leader. You may end up with one or more new groups for the course.

The housegroup leader's main responsibility is to ensure that tasks 2 and 3 are completed (see Group Sheet Week 1):

Beware of various pitfalls. For example, criticism of the church, criticism of the leadership and the downgrading of spiritual gifts.

a) Task 2. Each group member contributes something he/she found helpful from the talk. The group then decides the one most helpful point to bring back to the plenary session and the leader writes this down, ideally on an overhead projector slide.

b) Task 3. Each group member says what their question is. The group then decides on the one question it would like to ask in the plenary session and the leader writes it down, ideally on an overhead projector slide.

Arrange for someone to collect the helpful points and the questions ready for the plenary session.

ALL TOGETHER

Spend a short time inviting comments on the 'helpful points' but spend much more time on the questions. These give an 'agenda' and highlight items which people want to know more about. Ensure time is allowed for each question - how this is done clearly depends on the number of groups you have. It may be that a definitive answer cannot be given immediately - give a guarantee that the question will be covered in the course, and make sure that it is. Questions and Answers (page 38) may prove helpful.

The Minister can deal with questions in these ways:

1. You as minister give an answer.

2. Invite answers from accepted 'leaders' in the church.

3. Invite anyone to share from their experience.

4. A mixture of the above.

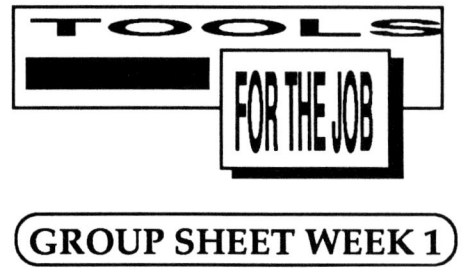

GROUP SHEET WEEK 1

TASK 1 (TO BE COMPLETED DURING THE TALK)

Write down what you believe your gifts are and how you are using them in the church and in the world.

TASK 2 (IN GROUPS)

Make a note of one thing from the talk which you found particularly helpful.

TASK 3 (IN GROUPS)

Make a note of any question(s) which came to mind as you listened to the talk.

© Copyright CPAS 1990 (P) Copying for group members is permitted

HANDOUT NOTES FOR KEYNOTE TALK WEEK 1

"THE GOD WHO GIVES GIFTS"

A. INTRODUCTION

1 In looking at spiritual gifts we are looking at a central New Testament theme which cannot be ignored. It is important to identify biblical principles which can then be developed in our local situation.

2 Jesus is Lord: He is the active leader of the local church. Gifts come from his hands and are given to us through the Holy Spirit (1 Cor 12:7).

3 All Christians are called by God to serve him. We are given different gifts, but these are to be shared among the Body of Christ. This picture of the 'Body' reminds us:

  a) all Christians matter 1 Cor 12: 14-16
  b) the whole range of gifting matters 1 Cor 12: 17-25

4 Gifts are not just for the church but for the world. They are the tools needed to reach out to a broken world. Many Christians are called to exercise their gifts in the world.

B. THE GIFTS OF THE SPIRIT (1 Cor 12: 4-7)

There are 5 key words/phrases:

1 **Gifts are Gifts of Grace** (charismata). v4 All Christians are "Charismatic" in that we live and exist in Christ by the grace of God. God's great charisma is eternal life (Rom 6: 23) - totally undeserved. Spiritual gifts are an outworking of this grace and must never be seen as a basis of pride (1 Cor 4: 7). God is able to work through new Christians though we need to become increasingly mature in Christ in order to use the gifts wisely.

2 **Gifts are for Service not Status.** We are to serve Jesus in his church/world. This leads to a mutual building up as we serve one another. Gifts ministered without a spirit of loving service are worthless (1 Cor 13: 1-3).

3 **Gifts are God Working** (energemata), v.6. When there is a genuine gift of the Spirit, something happens. For example, you do not have the gift of evangelism only if you like talking about Jesus: you have the gift if through you others are led to Christ. Gifts are not about feelings. They are about God's energy working through Christians so that something happens.

4 **Gifts are Manifestations of the Spirit**, v 7. Gifts are the Holy Spirit made visible. We cannot see him but we can see the evidence of his work (cf wind); we can see the difference he makes. To despise the gifts is to quench the Spirit.

5 **There are Varieties of Gifts**, v. 4-6 (see also 1 Peter 4: 10). There is a wide variety of gifts available to God's people (Rom 12: 6-8; 1 Cor 12: 4-11, 27-30; Eph 4: 11, 12).

The list contains both 'natural' and 'supernatural' gifts, though it is important to appreciate that the Bible never makes such a distinction. All gifts require human response and activity. God can take natural abilities and make them supernatural. (e.g. gift of the gab...gift of evangelism). We must be careful however, not to think it is enough just to have a natural gift. The coming of the Holy Spirit sharpens up natural gifts and puts them under the Lord's control but he also enables us to do those tasks that can only be accomplished through spiritual gifts.

No Christian has all the gifts and we need our ministry to be complemented by the ministry of others (Rom 12: 4,5).

We need to be open to whatever gift the Holy Spirit wants to give us. Gradually patterns of gifting will emerge as we discover God's particular gift(s) for us.

C. FINDING OUR GIFTS AND MINISTRIES

It is very important that we have the right church environment in order for the gifts to develop and flourish:

    a) a church with teaching and pastoral care

    b) a church with meaningful fellowship

    c) a church with commitment and love.

D. CONCLUSION

    Is God beginning to work in my life?

    Do other people see God at work in me?

    Do I really want God to work in my life?

    Dare I take the risk of beginning/stepping out in faith?

God gives power in weakness. What we have to do is ask and be ready to receive. *"If you then, though you are evil, know how to give good gifts to your children, how much more will your Father in heaven give the Holy Spirit to those who ask him"* (Lk 11: 13).

OUTLINE OF MINISTERS KEYNOTE TALK WEEK 1
"THE GOD WHO GIVES GIFTS"

A. INTRODUCTION

1 In looking at spiritual gifts we are looking at a central New Testament theme which cannot be ignored. It is important to identify biblical principles which can then be developed in our local situation.

Make it clear that you are seeking to find out what the Bible really says and not trying to sell any 'party-line'.

2 Jesus is Lord: He is the active leader of the local church. Gifts come from his hands and are given to us through the Holy Spirit (1 Cor 12: 7). It is important to take seriously the priority of the gift of the Spirit himself over the gifts of the Spirit. We need to 'keep on being filled' with the Spirit and so we ALL need to be seeking more of what God wants to give by his Spirit.

You may want to use material from The Message of Ephesians by John Stott (IVP - 'The Bible Speaks Today' series), especially commentary on ch 5: 18.

3 All Christians are called by God to serve him. We are given different gifts, but these are to be shared among the Body of Christ. This picture of the Body reminds us:
   a) All Christians matter
   b) The full range of gifting matters

Wagner's book lists 27 gifts of the Spirit covering a wide range. You may like to mention some of the 'unknown' but vital jobs that people do in your church.

4 Gifts are not just for the church but for the world. They are the tools needed to reach out to a broken world. Many Christians are called to exercise their gifts in the world.

The church needs to be seen as the 'nurture' place from which Christians go out to serve. The church is a good place to try out the gifts and we can safely make mistakes. Many of the gifts will be exercised in the community and in the places where Christians work. The examples of both Jesus and the apostles show that the main sphere of Christian ministry is the world not the church (Jn 10: 11-16; Lk 10: 1-12).

ACTIVITY: (5 mins) **Group Sheet Task 1** will be needed. Ask everyone present to spend a few moments writing down what they believe their gifts are and how they are using them. When they have done that, ask them to compare notes with a neighbour. If you introduce this fairly light-heartedly then no-one should feel intimidated. Encourage people to share with their neighbour why they believe they have a particular gift.

B. THE GIFTS OF THE SPIRIT (1 Cor 12: 4-7)

For a fuller description read: Ministry in the Local Church (page 39)
Uncover each heading if you are using a chart or overhead projector (see page 16).

There are 5 key words/phrases:

1. GIFTS ARE GIFTS OF GRACE, verse 4. The Greek word for gifts is 'charismata', literally Gifts of Grace. All Christians are 'charismatic' in that we live and exist in Christ by the grace of God. God's great charisma is eternal life (Rom 6: 23) - something totally undeserved. Spiritual gifts are an outworking of this grace and must never be seen as a reason for pride, status or significance (1 Cor 4: 7).

Receiving 'Gifts of Grace' is not a theory but an experience. It is not an attitude but a generous act of God. Paul experienced the grace of God on the Damascus road (Acts 9).

God is able to work through new and young Christians, though we need to become increasingly mature in Christ in order to use the gifts wisely.

You may like to mention the story of a ten-year-old who came forward during an open time of sharing and asked the leader to read out some verses from Scripture which he believed God had given him a few weeks earlier. Shortly afterwards an older Christian spoke and linked these verses to the sermon.

2. GIFTS ARE FOR SERVICE NOT STATUS, verse 5. We are to serve Jesus in his church/world. Gifts are the practical tools given to serve others. This leads to a mutual building up as we serve one another. Gifts ministered without a spirit of loving service are worthless (1 Cor 13: 1-3).

As Christians we are called to exercise a 'towel ministry' (Jn 13: 5-15). This can be a humbling experience. Tom Walker gives the example of a youth fellowship ready to do washing up (Renew Us By Your Spirit p.33 Hodder & Stoughton). There is a bishop who used to (and may still do so) keep a small towel in his cassock pocket as a reminder of what his ministry is all about.

3. GIFTS ARE GOD WORKING (energemata), verse 6. When there is a genuine gift of the Spirit something happens. Gifts are not about feelings. They are about God's energy working through Christians to change people or situations. For example, you do not have the gift of evangelism if you just like talking about Jesus: you have the gift if through you others are led to Christ.

See the way Peter Wagner talks about his discovery that he did not have the gift of evangelism ('Your Spiritual Gifts Can Help Your Church Grow' Peter Wagner MARC : pp 120-123).

4. GIFTS ARE MANIFESTATIONS OF THE SPIRIT, verse 7. Gifts are the Holy Spirit made visible. We cannot see the Spirit but we can see the difference he makes. To despise the gifts is to quench the Spirit.

For the Hebrews Wind and Spirit were the same word. In John 3 Jesus says explicitly the Spirit is like the wind. When the wind is blowing, its reality can be accepted without any knowledge of its origin or destination. When certain things happen in human life they give us real assurance that the Spirit has been at work (cf Acts 8:18; Gal 5:22, 23).

The hurricane of 1987 could be a good example to use if people in your area were affected. You could also challenge people to ask themselves 'What difference is there in my life now that I am a Christian? Is that difference seen by others?'

5   THERE ARE VARIETIES OF GIFTS, verses 4-6. (see also 1 Pet 4: 10). There is a wide variety of gifts available to God's people (Rom 12: 6-8; 1 Cor 12: 4-11; Eph 4: 11, 12).

Wagner lists 27 different gifts. (pp 259-263)

The gifts available appear to be both 'natural' and 'supernatural'. It is important to appreciate that the Bible never makes such a distinction. Divine initiative requires a human response. God can take a natural ability and turn it into a supernatural gift (for example Canon Harry Sutton speaks of how God changed the gift of the gab in his life into the gift of evangelism). However we must be careful not to assume automatically that our natural abilities will become our spiritual gifts.

Refer to 'Ministry in the Local Church' (page 39) and 'Gifts of the Spirit in the Local Church' (page 59) for further discussion on this issue.

No Christian has all the gifts and we need our ministry to be complemented by the ministry of others (Rom 12: 4, 5). We need to be open to whatever gift the Holy Spirit wants to give us. Gradually patterns of gifting will emerge as we discover God's particular gift(s) for us.

It may be worth pointing out the difference between a gift and a ministry. When a gift is being consistently used then it can be said to be a person's ministry. It may be that God gives us a gift for a particular occasion. For example, we may not have the gift of evangelism but if someone asks us how you become a Christian, and there is no-one else available, then it is highly likely that God will use us on that occasion.

C. FINDING OUR GIFTS AND MINISTRIES

It is very important that we have the right church environment in order for the gifts to develop and flourish:

a)   A church with teaching and pastoral care
b)   A church with meaningful fellowship
c)   A church with commitment and love

Teaching only takes place when people actually learn something.

All this demands shared, active leadership, not abdication of leadership. You may not want to develop this in your talk, but you should be aware of the implications. See 'Leadership in the Local Church' (page 49) for biblical references.

D. CONCLUSION

> Is God beginning to work in my life?
> Do others see God at work in my life?
> Do I really want God to work in my life?
> Dare I take the risk of beginning/stepping out in faith?

What we have to do is ask and be ready to receive. *'If you then, though you are evil, know how to give good gifts to your children, how much more will your Father in heaven give the Holy Spirit to those who ask him'* (Lk 11: 13).

THE GIFTS OF THE SPIRIT
for the Church and for the World

GIFTS ARE:-

GIFTS OF GRACE

FOR SERVICE NOT STATUS

GOD WORKING

MANIFESTATIONS OF THE SPIRIT

THERE ARE VARIETIES OF GIFTS

COURSE LEADER'S GUIDE

WEEK 2

"ALL RIGHT WITH GOD"

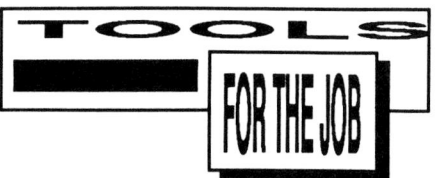

WEEK 2 "ALL RIGHT WITH GOD"

In Housegroups

OVERALL AIM

To examine the biblical material on gifts and to consider -

a)   what gifts people already have and need to work on

b)   what specific requests people have

NEEDED FOR THIS SESSION

1. Photocopies of Group Sheet Week 2 (for each member)

2. For the leader's talk see page 60, Finding our Gifts and Ministries (Resource Section 5 Gifts of the Spirit in the Local Church.)

3. Useful – 'Your Spiritual Gifts Can Help Your Church Grow' C Peter Wagner (MARC)

4. Two large sheets of paper to list ideas in tasks 2 and 4.

OUTLINE OF THE SESSION
Refer to Group Sheet Week 2

NOTES

The study looks at gifts in the Bible, and in the life of the church today, getting people familiar with the variety of God's provision as all kinds of needs arise.

A brief talk from the group leader is suggested based on Finding our Gifts and Ministries (page 60).

For the 'homework' assignment group leaders will find it especially helpful to have available for people Wagner's book. The definitions of various gifts are most useful (pages 259-263).

The 'homework' is optional (though important). Please ensure that no one is left feeling upset or unable to do this part of the course.

Work out in advance how long you intend to spend on each section. It is usually unhelpful to spend too much time on one task. You will probably find it impossible to cover all the material - BE SELECTIVE and try to meet the particular needs of your group.

GROUP SHEET FOR WEEK 2

"ALL RIGHT WITH GOD"

TASK 1:

We need to remind ourselves that when we look for God's gift it is crucial that we are "Right with God" in our attitude to his gifts and in our relationship with him.

Discuss together: Who is ultimately to benefit from receiving God's gifts? Is it the church? Is it the individual Christian? Is it God himself? Is it the world?
(Eph 4: 11, 12; Rom 12: 4, 5; 1 Pet 4: 10; 1 Pet 2: 9, 10)

Try to think of incidents in the Bible where there is a wrong attitude to God's gifts and his power. If you get stuck, try Acts 8: 9, 13, 18-24. What are the dangers for us in our attitude to God's gifts and his power?

What must our church be like in order to provide the best place for God's gifts to be received and used?
(Jn 13: 34; Rom 12: 9-13)

Your Group Leader will provide some material at this stage on finding our gifts and ministries.

TASK 2:

As a group make a list of spiritual gifts that are found in the Bible. You may like to add any that you have discovered from your own experience too.

TASK 3:

Divide into groups of three and take it in turns being in the hot seat. The other two people in the group will tell you what they believe your gifts are. The one rule is that people only say positive things. If you don't know the person well enough then simply say so.

TASK 4:

As a group you must now consider what gifts are needed in your church.

Make a list of those gifts which you feel are needed to run your church effectively. Put a mark next to those gifts which are in short supply or next to those activities which are short of leaders/helpers.

Check this list against the list made in Task 2. Are there any gifts mentioned in the Bible which ought to be evident in your church?

HOMEWORK (*THIS IS OPTIONAL*)

Each person should select one or two of the gifts you have identified and try to write out a brief definition of that gift. Can you think of any biblical examples to illustrate the use of this gift?

COURSE LEADER'S GUIDE

WEEK 3

"FOR WHAT WE ARE ABOUT TO RECEIVE"

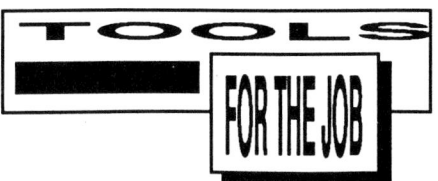

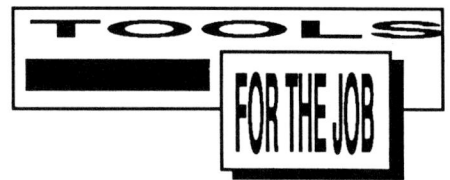

WEEK 3 "FOR WHAT WE ARE ABOUT TO RECEIVE"

In Housegroups

OVERALL AIM
To look further at some biblical teaching on spiritual gifts and to prepare for the following week's session when we come to receive from God and to rededicate ourselves to him.

NEEDED FOR THIS SESSION
1. Photocopies of Group Sheet Week 3 (for each member).
2. Especially helpful will be the definitions of spiritual gifts on pages 259-263 of Wagner.
3. Charts from Week 2.

OUTLINE OF THE SESSION
Refer to Group Sheet Week 3

NOTES
You will need to limit carefully the time spent on Task 1. Refer again to the advice in week 2 about being selective. See Page 61, A Way Forward (Resource Section 5. Gifts of the Spirit in the Local Church)

You might like to use the following illustration and questions to draw out some of the issues in Task 2.

The church youth group was being successfully run by a young married couple, Alan and Barbara, and they invited a student, Colin, to join them in the leadership team. Members of the group appeared to be growing spiritually and the Vicar was happy to leave the group in Alan and Barbara's hands. Following a weekend away it was revealed that Colin had brought some alcohol and had shared this with some of the youngsters at a late night party in his room. Alan and Barbara felt they had no option but to relinquish their position.

(a) Was the Vicar right to abdicate all responsibility for the group?
(b) What should happen to Colin in this situation? Was youth work his 'gift'?
(c) Alan and Barbara were gifted in youth work. Should this gift be lost as a result of this incident, or is there another solution? What about a ministry of encouragement?
(d) The session may raise the question of priorities in life. It has been suggested that our priorities in this situation should be:
   1. Me and God.
   2. Me and my partner.
   3. Me and my children.
   4. Me and others.

What are the implications of this in your personal life and in the life of your church for applying these priorities?

WE STRONGLY RECOMMEND THAT THE MINISTER AND HOUSEGROUP LEADERS MEET BETWEEN WEEKS 3 AND 4 IN ORDER TO PREPARE FOR SESSION 4. HOUSEGROUP LEADERS SHOULD BE FULLY SUPPORTIVE OF THE MINISTER AND SHOULD HAVE ENCOURAGED GROUP MEMBERS TO COME TO SESSION 4 IN A SPIRIT OF EXPECTANCY.

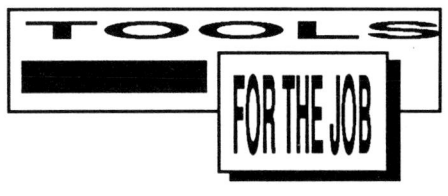

GROUP SHEET WEEK 3

"FOR WHAT WE ARE ABOUT TO RECEIVE"

TASK 1:

Group members have an opportunity to give their definition of the 'gift' selected at the end of last week's session. For each definition, ask these questions:

1. Is there anything to add to this definition?

2. Are there any restrictions on the use of this gift?

3. Can you think of any biblical examples to help in understanding the use of this gift?

4. Does anyone have any particular experience of the use of this gift?

5. Does Peter Wagner's definition (from his book 'Your Spiritual Gifts Can Help Your Church Grow') help any further? If you have this book see pages 259-263.

FOR PERSONAL REFLECTION

You may like to write down your personal reactions to this exercise. Make a note too of any gifts that are new to you and those you would like to explore further. Discuss this, if you like, with others.

TASK 2: TURNOVER

TASK 2

Study the following passages together:

a) **REKINDLE** (2 Tim 1: 6).

Read verse 7 to discover what the particular gift was.
Why do you think Paul said this to Timothy? (Look carefully at the context of this statement).

How can a Christian go about 'rekindling' a lost gift?

b) **RECEIVE** (1 Tim 4: 11-16, especially verse 14).

Think of occasions, especially in Acts, when people received gifts from God. The following passages may help you ... Acts 3: 1-10; 4: 36, 37; 13: 1, 2.

Think too of any occasions found in the Old Testament. For example,

Solomon (1 Kings 3: 10-28)

Samson (Judg 15: 14; Judg 16: 28-30)

What advice would you give a Christian who is seeking a gift from God?

c) **RESIGN** (or **RELINQUISH** or **RETURN TO THEIR GIVER**).

In 2 Tim 1: 11, 12 and 2 Tim 2: 9 Paul reminds us that he would have loved to have continued to exercise his gift of public preaching, but in prison he had to find new gifts - such as writing.

Can you think of any other examples from the Bible? (e.g. Philip, Acts 8: 4- 8, 26-40).

What happens when a person is, for example, finding that work or pressures at home make it impossible to have sufficient time to run, say, the youth group? Is this a time to resign and seek new areas of service?

FOR NEXT WEEK

Note here, as you prepare for Week 4 what your prayer is for yourself... to Rekindle, Receive or Resign.

Course Leader's Guide

WEEK 4

"GIFTS FROM GOD"

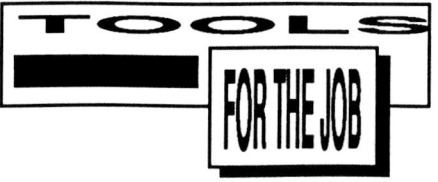

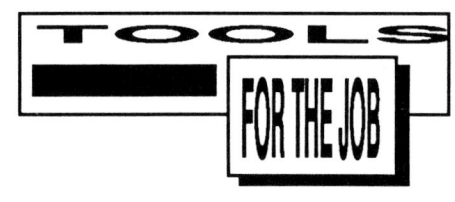

WEEK 4 "GIFTS FROM GOD"

All together, in church if appropriate. In preparing for this service, the meeting of housegroup leaders with the minister will provide information on how the groups are progressing and what particular questions need to be addressed.

OVERALL AIM
To worship together as the Body of Christ and to seek to discover what particular gifts God is wanting to give to your church at this particular time.

NEEDED FOR THIS SESSION
1. Church Family Worship (Hodder & Stoughton/Jubilate/CPAS)
2. Your own Service Sheet if you decide to have one
3. Useful–The Gifts of the Spirit in the Local Church (page 59).
4. Useful–Spiritual Gifts and Personal Ministry (page 57).
5. Useful–John Stott's comments on Ephesians 5:18 (*The Message of Ephesians* IVP, 'The Bible Speaks Today' series)
6. Overhead projector
7. Photocopies of Act of Commitment if required. (See page 27)

OUTLINE OF THE SESSION
The congregation will appreciate clear and firm leadership. Possible ways to develop the time together include:

1. Through a liturgical or informal Communion Service (see Church Family Worship items 15-47).
2. Renewal of baptismal vows, perhaps concentrating especially on the question: 'Do you believe and trust in his Holy Spirit, who gives life to the people of God?' (ASB pages 246/7).
3. Laying on of hands for individuals to receive particular gifts.
4. A non-eucharistic service, perhaps using some of the material in Church Family Worship items 302-327.

NOTES
If laying on of hands or renewal of baptismal vows are new ideas to your congregation, include substantial guidance either before the liturgy proper or as part of the ministry of the word.

The way you handle the service will depend on your previous experience, and that of your congregation. Some congregations will appreciate the corporate renewal of baptismal vows in a service based around the theme of commitment, while congregations which are used to praying for individuals with the laying on of hands will understand and appreciate this approach.

There is no Group Sheet this week but you may wish to provide a service sheet which could include:
1. Practical instructions about the service.
2. Notes on your talk.
3. Items for an informal service.
4. Act of commitment (example on page 27)
5. Covenant Service (Church Family Worship pages 25/6).

IT IS IMPORTANT THAT THE **TALK** IS INTEGRATED WITH THE REST OF THE COURSE AND THAT IT FITS IN WITH WHERE PEOPLE HAVE GOT TO.

THUS IT IS IMPORTANT THAT YOU KNOW HOW THE GROUPS ARE PROGRESSING. THE ITEMS LISTED IN "**NEEDED FOR THIS SESSION**" MAY HELP YOU IN YOUR PREPARATION.

ACT OF COMMITMENT

Reading: Philippians 3: 7-14

Quiet reflection and prayer.

Leader: Let those of us who wish to commit ourselves anew to the service of

Christ in .... and in the world, please stand.

Paul writes: 'I appeal to you brethren by the mercies of God to present yourselves as a living sacrifice, holy and acceptable to God, which is your spiritual worship. Do not be conformed to this world, but be transformed by the renewal of your mind, that you may prove what is the will of God, what is good and acceptable and perfect.

(Based on Romans 12 : 1, 2)

> 'Having gifts that differ according to the grace given to us, let us use them
> ... Let love be genuine; hate what is evil, hold fast to what is good
> ... Never flag in zeal, be aglow with the Spirit, serve the Lord.'

Do you present yourselves as living sacrifices?

All: **We present ourselves as living sacrifices;**
We are committed to the cause of Christ;
We are willing to serve.

Leader: Do you resolve, therefore, before God, depending on his Holy Spirit, to be faithful to this calling?

All: **By the help of God, we do.**

Leader: Will you then, in the strength of the Holy Spirit, continually stir up the gift that is in you, to bring the Kingdom of Christ to all and to build his church?

All: **By the help of God, we will.**

Leader: Will you now gather into threes and in turn pray briefly for one another, using the words that follow, or something similar. You may wish to accompany this by the laying on of hands.

(NAME) I pray for you that God the Father will strengthen you to trust him more, God the Son will lead you in his service, and God the Holy Spirit will equip you with power to love. **Amen.**

Leader: May God confirm his call in you
and strengthen you to do his will.
May you know the peace and power of God
as, with all the saints throughout the ages,
you overcome the Evil One.
Amen.

There is no group sheet for week 4.

COURSE LEADER'S GUIDE

WEEK 5

"EQUIPPING THE SAINTS"

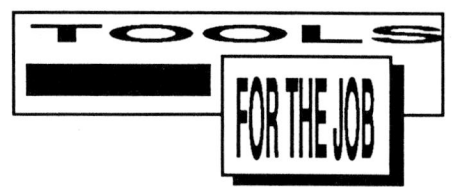

WEEK 5 "EQUIPPING THE SAINTS"

In Housegroups

OVERALL AIM
To provide an opportunity for personal testimony by group members and for them to encourage one another in their gifts. The study focuses on the work and ministry of individuals within the church and the needs which ought to be met through us as God equips.

NEEDED FOR THIS SESSION
1. Photocopies of Group sheet Week 5

2. Photocopies of Individual Assessment Sheet for group members (page 33)

3. Large sheets of paper for optional activity (or Photocopies of page 32)

4. Charts produced in weeks 2 and 3

OUTLINE OF THE SESSION
Refer to Group Sheet Week 5

There may be an opportunity to sort out any 'loose ends' and to gain feedback about the usefulness of the course. It would be a great help if leaders could encourage group members to complete the Individual Assessment Sheet (page 33). These should be studied locally to see if any lessons on leadership etc. emerge and then they should be forwarded to:
Vocation and Ministry Unit, CPAS, Falcon Court, 32 Fleet Street, London EC4Y 1DB.

This will ensure that future courses benefit from your reaction to this one.

The optional exercise based on 1 Corinthians 13 is recommended and a number of groups have found this to be a valuable activity (page 32).

NOTES
Work out how long you want to allow for Task 1. For example, if eight people speak for five minutes each then much of your time will have gone.

In Task 2 it may be worth saying that the needs of the local church are only a start. If people can cope with broadening the discussion at this point, include on your list some specific needs:

(i) in the local community
(ii) in our country
(iii) on the international scene

BE WATCHFUL FOR ANY MEMBER WHO APPEARS EITHER VERY QUIET OR RATHER CYNICAL OR NOT OPEN TO CHANGE. DO ANY MEMBERS APPEAR TO BE 'LEFT OUT' OF WHAT IS HAPPENING? YOU MAY FIND IT NECESSARY TO GET ALONGSIDE INDIVIDUALS IN ORDER TO HELP AND ENCOURAGE THEM.

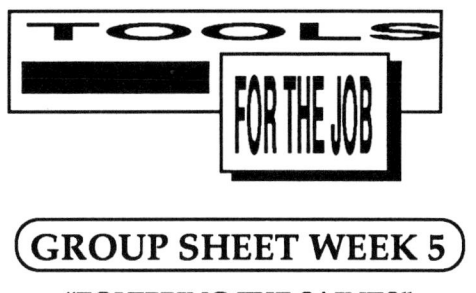

GROUP SHEET WEEK 5

"EQUIPPING THE SAINTS"

TASK 1:

Read Ephesians 4: 7, 8.

As a group spend some time recalling the previous week's experience, and what has happened since. Be sensitive to each other. Listen to what others are saying. Always encourage, don't criticise.

Is there anything you discovered last week that you would like to share?

Are there still issues that you would like to discuss further?

TASK 2:

Think back to week 2 when you compiled a list of gifts needed in the church. In the light of subsequent sessions, do you want to change the list in any way?

TASK 3:

Read Acts 6: 1-4; Nehemiah 4: 6-23; Exodus 18: 17-27.

What do you see as the particular needs of God's people in each of these situations? What gifts are required to meet these needs?

Now consider the particular needs of your church at this time. What gifts are needed to meet them?

© Copyright CPAS 1990 (P) Copying for group members is permitted

OPTIONAL EXTRA ....

Rewrite 1 Corinthians 13 to make a wall poster for your church. (Whether you ever display it or not is unimportant. The purpose of this activity is to translate God's word into our world and our priorities.)

To get you started, imagine Paul was writing to your church about the use and misuse of spiritual gifts, ministries and jobs in the church. Then rewrite the thirteen verses. For example, for a church where music rather than tongues is the elevated gift you might begin:

'If I am a member of the church choir and sing like the angels but have not love, I am nothing..'

Don't be afraid to have fun with this exercise. There can hardly have been anyone at Corinth who didn't smile at the thought of being described as a noisy gong or a clanging cymbal.

ONE CORINTHIANS THIRTEEN RE-WRITTEN FOR..(YOUR CHURCH)

Now pray together.
Thank God for the specific gifts each one has and ask for
humility and love in using them.

© Copyright CPAS 1990 (P) Copying for group members is permitted

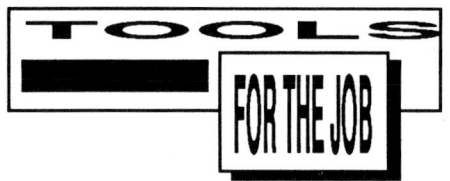

INDIVIDUAL ASSESSMENT SHEET

This sheet is in two halves. The top half is for you to keep and so is totally confidential. The bottom half is to tear off. It will help us to make sure that future courses benefit from your reactions to this one.

Write down in a list the key things:

You have learnt about God and yourself

1.

2.

3.

4.

You have decided to do differently as a result of the course

1.

2.

3.

4.

— — — — — — — — — tear off and hand in the portion below — — — — — — — — —

WHICH PARTS OF THE COURSE DID YOU FIND MOST HELPFUL?

Week 1	"The God who gives gifts"	A	B	C	D
Week 2	"All right with God"	A	B	C	D
Week 3	"For what we are about to receive"	A	B	C	D
Week 4	"Gifts from God"	A	B	C	D
Week 5	"Equipping the Saints"	A	B	C	D
Week 6	"Moving On"	A	B	C	D

Please circle   A– helpful
B– quite helpful
C– satisfactory but I did not learn anything new
D– unhelpful

Any comments: (continue over the page)

© Copyright CPAS 1990 (P) Copying for group members is permitted

COURSE LEADER'S GUIDE

WEEK 6

"MOVING ON"

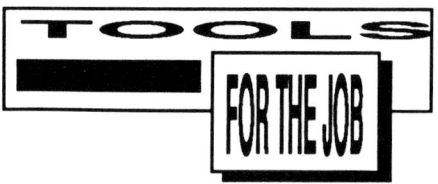

WEEK 6 "MOVING ON"

All together

OVERALL AIM

To provide an opportunity for the Minister to outline the way forward for introducing a gift-based ministry in the life of the church.

NEEDED FOR THIS SESSION

It is impossible to be too specific, because each church must move forward in its own way. Certainly lots of prayer!

OUTLINE OF THE SESSION

The evening could include:

1. Prayer and praise. The form this takes will naturally vary from church to church.

2. Testimony by church members who have been particularly encouraged by the course.

3. Talk based on 2 Tim 1:6 'For...I remind you to fan into flame the gift of God, which is in you.' (NIV)

    You might care to use the equations:

    GROWTH = CHANGE + PAIN   and   GROWTH = CHANGE + JOY

4. Explanation by Minister/church leader as to how you see future strategy regarding every member ministry.

Any process used needs to move your church from a system of involvement of people based on availability/status etc. to one based on spiritual giftedness. You are seeking to help people discover what God has designed for them to do and to give them an opportunity to do it. Members will be able to exercise areas of ministry for which they have been equipped by the Holy Spirit. Remember the goal is not simply to get people involved or to 'fill the gaps', but prayerfully to guide members into areas of service for which their gifts and background best equip them. The result will be that your congregation really does operate as the Body of Christ.

This is easy to say and not so easy to implement. IT WILL TAKE TIME to re-organise your church into gift-centred ministry and so it is crucial that you move ahead at a pace which is right for your church. Considerable re-education of members is needed (hopefully 'Tools for the Job' will have begun this process). Don't forget that people may need to 'try out' a job to see if God has equipped them for it.

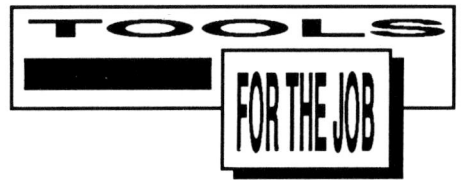

Resource Sections

1. QUESTIONS AND ANSWERS

Below are a few of the questions which arose when Graham Cray led a CPAS training day in Cambridge on 'Spiritual Gifts'. We have tried to summarise some of his points and to include some possible material of our own. Obviously it will depend on your local situation as to the depth to which you want to take any questions.

How do you distinguish between human talent and spiritual gifts?

- Work together so that there is mutual accountability. Learn *together* how to recognise God's gifting.

- Learn by experience, but be prepared to take risks with what people offer. People will gradually develop an awareness of how God works/speaks/reveals himself.
See 'Gifts of the Spirit in the Local Church ' (page 59)
See 'Ministry in the Local Church' (page 39)

How do you combine directive leadership with spiritual freedom?

- The leaders must be prepared to listen to what God is saying to them i) individually and ii) corporately and then act. (DIRECTIVE) They must also be prepared to listen to what God is saying through the words and deeds of the congregation (FREEDOM).
See 'Leadership in the Local Church' (page 49)

How do you deal with people who claim to have a gift, but clearly don't?

- Someone like this may be stubborn and refuse to listen. There are times when it is necessary to exercise discipline/authority for the well-being of the whole Body. However, we must be sensitive with people who genuinely believe they have a gift and ensure that they receive special pastoral care.
See 'Ministry in the Local Church' (page 39)

How do you deal with conflict between Minister and laity?
(e.g. Minister wants to move forward, congregation does not, and vice versa)

- 1 Corinthians 13 is a good place to begin.
- Build a greater sense of corporateness. Learn to value and trust one another. Minister needs to pray that God will show him those who are being gifted.
- Hold open meetings and thereby avoid cliques.

Is shared leadership possible in the Anglican church?

- As well as the PCC it may be right to create an Eldership or Ministry Team but seek PCC approval. Do not by-pass the PCC.
- In the NT leadership is always plural. (Acts 14: 23; Acts 20: 17ff)
- Leaders will be those of proven worth: all you are doing is acknowledging an authority already in evidence.
- Encourage those who are gifted in leadership to take up this role. Do not give the impression that 'up-front' gifts are superior to others.
See 'Leadership in the Local Church' (page 49)

How can I receive spiritual gifts?

- First, accept that this is God's work and that we are his co-workers. God wants to gift individual members in order to strengthen the Body and extend the Kingdom.
- Live a life of obedience to the Scriptures.
- Ask and (keep on asking) Luke 11: 9-13.
See 'Gifts of the Spirit in the Local Church' (page 59)

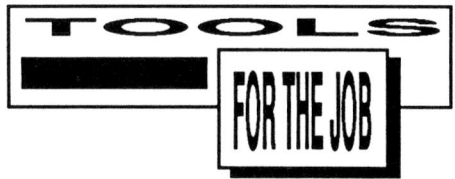

2. MINISTRY IN THE LOCAL CHURCH - THE GIFTS OF THE SPIRIT

Graham Cray

The gifts of the Spirit are the tools God gives to his people for their part in establishing his Kingdom. They are God's way of building up the church and continuing the ministry of Jesus to the world. They are the tangible ways in which we minister our life in Christ to one another and to the society in which we live. Without them there is no ministry and no mission. It is essential that they be properly understood.

THE SOURCE OF GIFTS

All ministry and mission originates from Christ. He builds his church (Mt 16:18). He commissions his servants (Mt 28:18-20). He sends the Spirit by whom we acknowledge that he is Lord (1 Cor 12:3, Acts 2:33). 'There is only one Christian ministry, that of Christ manifested through Christians.'[1] He gives the gifts of the Spirit (Eph 4:8), our gifts are the measure of his gift to us (Eph 4:7). His gifts are given to each Christian (1 Cor 12:7). The work of ministry and mission is the work of 'ordinary' believers, 'the saints' (Eph 4:12). The gifts of the Spirit are the tangible expression of the active leadership of the Lord Jesus in a congregation.

THE GIFTS IN CONTEXT

Any biblical study of the gifts of the Spirit must take into account the overall picture of corporate life in Christ which the New Testament portrays. Robert Banks has written that in the Pauline churches 'the focal point of reference was neither a book ... nor a rite, but a set of relationships and that God communicated himself to them primarily...through one another.' [2]

1. **Fellowship** (koinonia) eg 2 Cor 13:14, Phil 2:1, etc. Underlying concept: generous sharing, a shared life. We share in the Holy Spirit (2 Cor 13:14, Phil 2:1), in the grace of God (Phil 1:7), in the gospel (Phil 1:5), in God's nature (2 Pet 1:4), in future glory (1 Pet 5:1), in each other's sufferings (2 Cor 1:7), in the suffering of Christ (Phil 3:10) and in his body and blood at Holy Communion (1 Cor 10:16-17).

2. **The Family of God.** In Christ we are the children of a heavenly Father and the Spirit is given to assure us of our sonship (Rom 8:14-16, Gal 4:6-7). Our security and status is that we are sons of God and is based on God's free acceptance of us in Christ; not on the level of our 'performance', gifts or status. As sons and daughters of God we are to regard one another as brothers and sisters, family in the fullest sense. We must accept love, give and be committed to one another to the full extent of Christ's love for us (Col 3:12-17, 1 Peter 1:22, 1 John 3:10-18, 4:7-21, etc).

3. **The Body of Christ.** Paul's understanding of the church as the Body of Christ is that it is an *organism*, not just an *organisation*. Not just a matter of sharing out responsibilities, tasks and leadership, but of genuine interdependence. We are 'members one of another' (Rom 12:5). 'If one member suffers, all suffer together' (1 Cor 12:26). We are to 'weep with those who weep and rejoice with those who rejoice' (Rom 12:15). The gifts and ministries of 1 Corinthians 12 and 14 are only valid when shared in the context of the depth of love described in 1 Corinthians 13. They have been described as 'the living movements of Christ's Body'.

It is vital that the New Testament understanding of the Christian faith as a 'shared life' is grasped, otherwise the teaching on gifts is seen at worst as the basis for a parish 'talent register', and at most as shared responsibility without mutual commitment and openness.

THE NATURE OF SPIRITUAL GIFTS

Five words in 1 Cor 12:4-7 give a clear insight into the nature of the gifts of the Holy Spirit. Each is applicable to all gifts and together they amount to a multiple definition.

1 Gifts (charismata), v 4

Every moment and every aspect of the Christian life is an experience of the grace of God. Ministry is no exception. The gifts (*charismata*) of the Holy Spirit are gifts of grace (*charis*). In the New Testament grace is not a theoretical doctrine, but is always in action and experience. 'For Paul, grace does not mean an attitude or disposition of God; it denotes rather the wholly generous *act* of God'. [3] We are saved and upheld by grace; as we often sing, 'tis grace that brought me safe thus far and grace will lead me home.' The *charisma* of God is eternal life itself (Rom 6:23), and the gifts of the Spirit are specific manifestations of that life to uphold and upbuild the local church. Eternal life was revealed in Jesus, so as to be seen, heard and touched (1 John 1:1-2). Similarly the gifts of the Spirit apply the life of God tangibly to situations of need or opportunity in and through the Body of Christ. James Dunn has defined a spiritual gift as 'any word or act which embodies grace'. [4] This identification of spiritual gifts as manifestations of grace is so specific that the NT sometimes uses the word grace (*charis*) in place of the word gift (*charisma*). Sometimes the two words are used in parallel (1 Peter 4:10, Rom 12:6).

On occasions however, the word grace is used to mean specific gift or calling. In Eph 3: 7-8, Paul speaks of the specific gift and calling he has received for ministry to the Gentiles. The identification of gift and calling is easy to grasp because God does not call to specific service without also equipping for the task. Paul described the giving of this gift as an act of God's power. His use of the word 'grace' in this context implies far more than the graciousness of God in calling 'the chief of sinners' to be an evangelist. The gift he received is a specific manifestation of grace to empower for service. (See also Rom 12:3 where Paul's claim to authority is on the basis of his 'grace' - gift - as a leader.) In the introduction to 1 Corinthians Paul's thanksgiving that the Corinthian believers 'are not lacking in any spiritual gift' (1:7) is 'because of the grace of God which was given you in Christ Jesus' (1:4).

If spiritual gifts are manifestations of grace, a number of conclusions follow. First, every Christian is charismatic because every Christian is saved and upheld by grace. The 'charismatic movement' may only use that title (which many of us dislike) in the sense that it is a renewal movement, calling the church to act according to its true nature; not in the sense of any exclusive claim to the charismatic realm.

Second, if spiritual gifts are manifestations of the grace of God, they are not to be precisely identified with the natural or creation-given abilities. They amount to more than a local church talent list. The question of the 'natural' and 'supernatural' in gifts will be dealt with below. Some are indeed natural abilities empowered by the Spirit through the call of Christ, but not all spiritual gifts are 'anointed talents' and certainly not all natural talents become spiritual gifts.

Third, if they are experiences of grace, they are undeserved and are no guarantee of maturity and give no grounds for pride. 'What have you that you did not receive? If then you received it, why do you boast as if it were not a gift?' (1 Cor 4:7)

2 Service (diakonia), v 5

The gifts of the Spirit are acts of service. They are always for others. They exist solely to 'build up' the body of Christ (1 Cor 14:12, Eph 4:12). Paul longed to come to Rome 'to impart to you some spiritual gift *to strengthen you* (Rom 1:11). The only gift which is for personal upbuilding is the private use of tongues (1 Cor 14:4) through which I am strengthened to be a servant of my Lord and my brothers. Gifts 'ministered' without a spirit of loving service are worthless (1 Cor 13:1-3). In the NT the words 'minister' and 'ministry' apply not so much to a position, status, job description or pattern of activity as to the inner desire to serve, empowered and led by the Spirit, in response to Christ's call. Even in the Pastoral Epistles, where formal titles and patterns of leadership are emerging, Paul uses the same root word for service to describe his ministry, that of Timothy, and the title 'deacon' (1 Tim 1:12, 3:8, 4:6).

3 Workings (energemata), v 6

When there is a genuine gift of the Holy Spirit something happens. God does something. He is at work through a Christian. The gifts are not personal emotional experiences, they are acts of God's power achieving his purposes. If someone has a gift of evangelism he will lead people to Christ. Paul describes his receiving of a gift as a working of God's power (Eph 3:7). The genuine nature of the gift was confirmed by the fruitfulness of his ministry (Rom 15:15-19). His converts were his letters of recommendation (2 Cor 3:2). In the same way, if there is a gift of healing, someone is healed, at least partially. (Each healing is an individual gift of the Spirit, just as each conversion is an individual gift of evangelism, etc.) Where there is a gift of teaching, believers will come to a new understanding and experience of biblical truth. The same principle applies to the whole range of gifts. They are acts of the Holy Spirit through Christians.

4 Manifestations of the Spirit, v 7

The gifts are the Spirit made visible, his reality and presence demonstrated. The Holy Spirit exercising his role as the primary witness to the resurrection of Jesus (Jn 15:26, Rom 15:18-19, 1 Cor 2:1-5, Heb 2:4, etc). They are the outworking of the Spirit-filled life. To ask to be filled with the Holy Spirit without being willing to minister spiritual gifts is a *non sequitur*. It is to ask for an emotional experience which makes no practical difference to ministry or mission. Similarly to forbid, despise or refuse to minister the gifts of the Spirit is to quench the Holy Spirit (1 Thess 5:19-22).

5 Varieties, vv 4-6

We are to be 'good stewards of God's *varied* grace' (1 Peter 4:10). Each believer has been given at least one gift of the Holy Spirit (Rom 12:6, 1 Cor 7:7, 12:7, Eph 4:7, 1 Peter 4:10), but there is a wide variety of gifts and we are not all given the same (1 Cor 12:4-11). The NT writers assume that we know what our gifts are, when they tell us to use them. (Sadly not an assumption they could automatically make today.) The ministry of the Spirit is also to help us to understand the gifts (1 Cor 12). Only the 'unspiritual' Christian does not understand them (1 Cor 2:12, 3:1-4). There are lists of gifts in Romans 12:6-8, 1 Cor 12:8-10, 28-30, Eph 4:11, 1 Peter 4:9-11, as well as other individual gifts mentioned in other passages. The lists include utterance of wisdom, utterance of knowledge, faith, healing, miracles, prophecy, the ability to distinguish between spirits, tongues, interpretation of tongues, apostles, prophets, evangelists, pastors and teachers, helpers, administrators, exhortation, giving, acts of mercy, hospitality and celibacy (1 Cor 7:7). All are gifts of the Holy Spirit to the church. Sometimes they are described in terms of their function (eg healing), sometimes the person through whom the function is ministered is called the gift (eg 'teacher'). The various lists overlap and some of the descriptions are fairly general.

Rather than being in watertight compartments, the various gifts merge into one another like the colours of the rainbow. There is no indication that the lists are intended to be comprehensive. They appear to be cross sections of the possibilities. If a gift of the Spirit is indeed 'any word or act which embodies grace' then the possibilities are limitless. Jürgen Moltmann put it well: 'The energies of new life in the Spirit are as manifold and motley as creation itself. Nothing is to be passed over, pushed aside or given up. On the contrary, everything is to be made eternally alive. That is why Paul talks about the *charismata* with such assurance. They overflow with an abundance whose extent cannot be fixed once and for all...In principle every human potentiality and capacity become charismatic through a person's call, if only they are used in Christ.' [5] Indeed, to be true to the breadth of the New Testament we need to go further. If *the* charismatic gift is eternal life, the whole of life in every area becomes the realm of spiritual gifts, as Moltman says. Our daily conversations are to 'edify' others and 'impart grace' (the specific functions of spiritual gifts) rather than 'grieve the Spirit' (Eph 4:29-30). But it is not just that any 'natural' creation - given ability may be empowered by the Spirit to be a spiritual gift. The Spirit is also described as 'the powers of the age to come' (Hebrews 6:4-5). Gifts like miracles, healing, prophecy and tongues, those that are apparently more 'supernatural', are demonstrations of this aspect of God's kingdom. As in the ministry of Jesus the power of the future kingdom is experienced today, for Jesus said that the works he did we would do (Jn 14:12).

The distinction between 'natural' and 'supernatural' is not a biblical one. The New Testament lists mix the two categories with abandon. Each gift involves the 'natural' and the 'supernatural'. 'All charisms involve divine initiative in the midst of thoroughly human activity.' [6] An apparently 'natural' gift like administration needs the anointing of the Spirit if it is to order rather than stifle the life of the Spirit in the church. Canon Harry Sutton has said that he was born with 'the gift of the gab' and that God turned it into a gift of evangelism. Sadly, there are many Christians with the gift of the gab used only for destructive purposes. Our natural abilities only become gifts of the Spirit under the specific calling and anointing of God. Similarly the apparently more supernatural gifts involve 'thoroughly human activity'. A gift of healing requires a voice to pray, and often hands to be laid on or to anoint with oil. A prophecy requires vocal chords to speak it out. The speaker in tongues has the control of the gift. He exercises his will and his vocal chords but trusts God for the words and sounds, rather than consciously creating them in ordinary speech.

Eternal life means that the power of the age to come has broken into our everyday existence, making everything eternally alive. Spiritual gifts minister this to others in tangible ways. Arnold Bittlinger has written, 'For the charismatic (every reborn Christian is a charismatic) there is no longer a boundary between this world and the world beyond. He views God and the world as realms that he can no longer separate from one another, not even in himself.' [7]

Because there is such a vast range of gifts, sovereignly distributed by the Spirit, we are not to be envious of the gifts of others or despise our own gifts (1 Cor 12:14-26). No Christian has all the gifts (1 Cor 12:29ff) and every Christian needs his ministry complemented by that of others (Rom 12:4-5). As the gifts are to build up the church, we are to desire and actively seek those which are most effective for that purpose (1 Cor 12:31, 14:1-12).

THE TESTING OF GIFTS

If ministry is gift based, then clearly the testing, weighing or judging of gifts is of vital importance. This should operate on three levels. (1) The leadership of the church has been given the gift and ministry of 'ruling' or being an 'overseer' (1 Tim 5:17, Acts 20:28, etc). This applies as much to the ministry of gifts as to any other aspect of church life. Those who minister are to be under the authority of the leaders and the leadership should give clear guidance to the fellowship about any major utterance and about the ministry of gifts in general. (2) Those who are mature in a particular gift have a special responsibility to weigh that gift when used by others and to submit their ministry to the correction of their peers (eg prophecy 1 Cor 14:29-30, teaching Acts 18:24-26, Titus 1:9). (3) The whole congregation has a personal responsibility to 'test all things and hold fast to what is good' (1 Thess 5:19-22).

The testing of the gifts like prophecy, interpretation of tongues, word of knowledge is particularly important (1 Thess 5:19-21, 1 Jn 4:1). A genuine gift of the Spirit will conform to the letter and spirit of Scripture, which is the ultimate test of content. There are a number of important criteria about the manner of delivery. Is the speaker in control of himself? (1 Cor 14:30-32) Is the message presented 'in love'? (1 Cor 13:2) Is the timing appropriate? Is the speaker open to correction and the gift presented so that others can judge? Is Jesus exalted or the speaker? What do you know of the speaker's life? (Mt 7:15ff) Is he speaking beyond his faith? (Rom 12:6) Does he speak beyond the prompting of the Holy Spirit? Stopping as well as starting needs to be inspired by the Spirit. Is the message appropriate to the situation? Is the speaker saying what you would expect him to say anyway? Is he speaking from prior knowledge? Is the speaker rooted in the life of the church?

There should also be an assessment of the results of the gift: did the members of the congregation have an inner conviction that they were hearing the voice of the Spirit? Did the message build up the church or just give someone a voice? If there was any prediction was it fulfilled? What were the long term consequences of previous messages?

GIFTS, MINISTRIES AND OFFICES

The New Testament material about the distribution of gifts and ministries in the church is complex, and it is not possible to be absolutely certain about the pattern suggested here, but I wish to make four points:

(1) Under the inspiration of the Holy Spirit any Christian may exercise any gift of the Spirit at any time. Just because we are told that each has a specific gift or gifts, we may not limit the sovereignty of the Holy Spirit to work through each in other ways as the need demands. Each child of God is to be open to the whole range of the Spirit's ministry. In this sense of the word, each action or word empowered by and directed by the Spirit is a spiritual gift. I may only minister healing once in my whole Christian life, but that would still be a gift of the Spirit. The Spirit distributes gifts according to the needs and opportunities of the Body of Christ and each of us needs to be open to the unexpected.

(2) However, the New Testament is clear that each Christian has been given a specific gift or gifts, that he is to know what it is and to use it. It may be easier to speak of a 'ministry' when referring to the consistent long term use of a specific gift, and 'gift' to refer to each specific occurrence.

Certainly, when referring to the consistent use of gifts, Paul often refers to the person, speaking of 'prophets', 'teachers', 'administrators', 'workers of miracles', 'he who exhorts', etc. Whatever the terminology, it is clear that each member of the Body of Christ should be able to give a straightforward answer to the question, 'What are your spiritual gifts?'

(3) Some of the titles (apostles, prophets, pastors, teachers, evangelists, etc [eg Eph 4, Acts 13]) seem to imply more than the consistent use of certain gifts. There are leadership roles in the local or wider church. There is no exact New Testament tie up

beween titles like 'elder', 'bishop' or 'deacon' and those which are also the name of gifts, but clearly in the New Testament leadership ministries, like all ministry, are gift-based. The authority of the leader is based on the gifts and calling of God in his life, not on status or position.

The ministry of 'apostle' and 'prophet' are no longer with us in the foundational sense of establishing doctrine or giving new revelation. We now have the New Testament in their place. However, the apostle continues in the sense of the ministry in the wider church. The ministry of the prophet also continues at both local church and wider church levels.

(4) If the basis of ministry is gift and if each believer has to be open to the initiative and direction of the Spirit, the structures of the local church must be appropriately flexible. Howard Snyder has written, 'The Church is marked by community, inter-personal relationships, mutuality and interdependence. It is flexible and leaves room for a high degree of spontaneity.' [8] It is the responsibility of the leaders to provide the structures and conditions in which the life and gifts of the Spirit may flourish and mature.

THE NURTURE AND RECOGNITION OF GIFTS

The leadership gifts (apostles, prophets, evangelists, pastors and teachers) are given to equip the saints for ministry (Eph 4:11-12). Traditional evangelical thinking has identified ministry almost entirely with teaching, pastoring and evangelism (often through one man). In the New Testament these ministries are the ones through which ordinary believers are equipped to exercise the whole range of spiritual gifts, which make up ministry.

1 Teaching (and Pastoral Care)

The teaching ministry must have a central place in the life of any church. Every part of the Christian life, individual and corporate, must be ordered by the Scriptures. Teachers need to follow the example of Paul who 'did not shrink from declaring anything that was profitable, teaching in public and from house to house' (Acts 20:20). The mark of a gift of the Spirit is that it builds up the Body of Christ and Paul describes the teaching ministry as 'the word of God's grace which is able to build you up' (Acts 20:32). Christians need an overall grasp of 'the whole counsel of God' (Acts 20:27), a doctrinal framework which enables them to have a scriptural balance about their understanding of Christian truth. It is not enough to know that a certain teaching is biblical. We need to know how it relates to the whole body of doctrine. It is only too easy to press one facet of truth to the point where it seems to exclude other emphases of the Bible.

A teaching ministry needs to be backed up with personal pastoral care. Indeed Eph 4:11 may imply that 'pastor and teacher' is one gift, rather than a pair of closely associated gifts. Paul exercised both ministries. 'I did not cease night or day to admonish everyone with tears' (Acts 20:31), 'warning every man and teaching every man in all wisdom, that we may present every man mature in Christ. For this I toil, striving with all the energy which he mightily inspires within me.' (Col 1:28-29)

The teaching ministry of a church should include regular instruction about the gifts of the Holy Spirit. Ministry will not develop if it is not taught. We only expect from God what we see promised in the Bible. Teaching instructs and builds faith to receive.

2 Building Fellowship

Although the gifts of the Spirit are exercised by individuals, they are gifts to the Body of Christ, gifts to an interdependent community. They need the setting of intimate fellowship both to emerge and to mature. It is the responsibility of leaders to encourage that fellowship.

All true believers are united in Christ. There is one body and one Spirit. The unity of the Spirit needs to be maintained, not created (Eph 4:3-6). Christians have a common participation (*koinonia*) in the Spirit (2 Cor 13:13-14, Phil 2:1). Through the cross and by the Spirit we are brothers and sisters and must treat each other accordingly. The gifts of the Spirit make us interdependent. None of us have all the gifts. Each of us needs his ministry complemented by that of others. Together we are the Body of Christ. Individually we are members of it, limbs, cells or organs (1 Cor 12:27); the gifts, the living movements of the body. Limbs and organs have no useful function apart from the body to which they belong, but the temptations to act as though I do not need others, or as though I do not count and am unnecessary, are very strong and need to be overcome by long-term teaching and pastoral care (1 Cor 12:12-26). Paul teaches that the members of the body *are* inter-dependent (for good or for ill), not that they should be. 'If one member suffers, all suffer together, if one member is honoured, all rejoice together' (v 26), 'We though many are one body in Christ, and individually members of one another' (Romans 6:5). As brothers and sisters, as members of the same Body we are to minister to one another, 'addressing one another in psalms and hymns and spiritual songs' (Eph 5:19), 'teach and admonish one another in all wisdom' (Col 3:16), 'exhort one another every day' (Heb 3:13), etc. The meetings of believers are to be marked by the contribution of each member (1 Cor 14:26ff).

This type of mutual ministry only functions in the context of deep, mutual commitment. Love is the context in which the gifts of the Spirit flourish. We are to love one another as Christ has loved us (Jn 13:34). In other words a total commitment to the point of death (Jn 13:1,14-15). We are to take the initiative in making relationships, just as he did with us (1 Jn 4:10-11). We are to risk rejection as he did. We have no right to wait until our brother or sister appears more responsive or takes the first step, for Christ died for us when we were sinners, helpless and his enemies (Rom 5:6-10). Equally we have no right to withold forgiveness from any Christian, for we have been forgiven (Mt 6:12-15, Eph 4:32, Col 3:13). When a relationship is broken we are to take the initiative in restoring it, whether we or the other person are primarily at fault (Mt 5:23-24, 18:15ff). We are to serve one another in practical ways (Jn 13:14-15) with our words (Eph 4:29, Heb 3:13, 10:24-25), with the sharing of our possessions and the generosity of our giving (Acts 4:32-37, 2 Cor 8, 9, 1 Jn 3:16-18), with the use of our homes, meeting together often (Heb 10:25, 1 Pet 4:9). Above all we are to be open with one another, sufficiently free to share ourselves (1 Thess 2:8) and identify deeply with the joys and pains of others (Rom 12:15-16, 1 Cor 12:25-26). We are to be those who regard themselves as being here for the Lord and for others. This quality of fellowship is summed up by Moltmann as follows:

- that no one is alone with his or her problems
- that no one has to conceal his or her disabilities
- that there are not some who have the say, and others who have nothing to say
- that neither the old nor the little ones are isolated
- that one bears the other even when it is unpleasant and there is no agreement
- that the one can also at times leave the other in peace when the other needs it. [9]

Relationships of this depth are part of our inheritance in the Spirit, but they do not appear overnight. I will not share myself with a person I do not trust. Trust requires knowledge of one another through meeting together over a length of time. Many of us need healing from past hurt and the effects of past sin before we can love others freely. Most Western Christians are conditioned by society to be independent rather than interdependent and such attitudes die slowly. Local church leaders may need to teach, counsel and pray over a long period before they see great progress. Often this teaching is quickly grasped at a superficial level, resulting in an appearance of fellowship, which is largely an ideal or fantasy without the costliness of Christian love, the love which took Jesus to the cross for us. Bonhoeffer gives a penetrating assessment of this type of fantasy in *Life Together*: 'Inumerable times a whole Christian community has broken down because it had sprung from a wish dream. The serious Christian, set down for the first time in a Christian community, is likely to bring with him a very definite idea of what Christian life together should be and try to realise it. But God's grace speedily shatters such dreams. Just as surely God desires to lead us to a knowledge of genuine Christian fellowship, so surely must we be overwhelmed by a great genuine disillusionment with others, with Christians in general, and, if we are fortunate, with ourselves. By sheer grace God will not permit us to live even for a brief period in a dream world'. [10] In a similar vein, Gerald Coates has said that Christian relationships go through three stages, veneer, disillusion and commitment. The middle stage of disillusion is essential. We have to reach the point in our relationships where we *have* to rely on the Holy Spirit, where what each of us is is fully known, yet we are still loved, accepted, forgiven and trusted. In the context of such love, gifts blossom and there we mature in their use, for we are not afraid to speak and act in God's name in each other's company. The body is built up when the gifts are ministered, but they are only authentic when ministered in love (1 Cor 13) and the only true growth is in love (Eph 4:16).

Clearly, the kind of meeting outlined in 1 Cor 14:26ff and similar passages requires a gathering sufficiently small, intimate and informal for each member present to contribute. A church of any size will require some sort of network of small groups if it is going to pay more than lip service to every member ministry. A useful distinction may be made between commitment and intimacy. I am called to be committed to every fellow-member of my congregation, however large it may be, as a matter of the will. Intimacy is only possible with a relatively small number and some form of fellowship group will be necessary for it to develop in a disciplined way.

3 The Initiative of Leaders

Spiritual gifts develop in the local church through teaching, which instructs the understanding and builds faith to appropriate what God offers, through the building up of the environment of fellowship in which they flourish and through the initiative and action of leaders in recognising and 'imparting' gifts. The leadership ministries of Eph 4:11 are to equip the saints for ministry. Sometimes leaders will receive guidance from the Spirit about new callings or changes in the ministry of certain individuals, as in Acts 13:1-3. However, it should be pointed out that, in this example, those who received this revelation included those who were involved, and the guidance was simply a matter of the timing of a response to a call already received from God. There was no question of 'ordering' people to do what they had not heard God tell them to do. Often leaders will discern the gift(s) that God is giving or has given to a particular Christian through the use of the 'word of knowledge' and will tell them, or pray for them, or often commission them through the laying on of hands. Timothy received a spiritual gift in this way, through Paul's ministry (2 Tim 1:6-7). We have already seen the relevance of the gifts of teaching and pastoral care in this field, but often the gift of prophecy has particular effect, with a direct word from God calling a believer to a specific ministry, or imparting a specific gift. Timothy also had this experience: 'do not neglect the gift you have, which was given you by prophetic utterance when the council of elders laid their hands upon you' (1 Tim 4:14). It is possible that Timothy had received a gift of evangelism but was tempted not to use it through timidity (see 1 Tim 4:11-13, 2 Tim 1:6-7, 4:5). These passages are often spoken of as referring to Timothy's 'ordination' but status and 'official position' in the New Testament only exists on the basis of a call of God and the ministry of the relevant gifts.

Often the gifts of individuals will be obvious to their fellows, even to the whole church, before they are convinced themselves (Acts 6:3). The initiative of leaders, exercising their own gifts to impart gifts has a vital role to play.

4 The Individual's Responsibility

Because the gifts are given to individuals (for the common good) it is the responsibility of each member of the church to receive, understand and use the gifts apportioned by the Spirit. Sometimes this comes through a growing awareness that God is using one in a particular way, or calling to a particular area of service. Often however, the certainty only comes in the doing. The gifts are words and actions, not feelings. Just as a child learns to walk or swim or ride a bike by doing it and acquiring balance and competence in the doing, so it is with the gifts of the Spirit. 'Having gifts that differ according to the grace given to us, let us *use* them' (Rom 12:6). An act of faith is needed to begin. Many of the gifts function on an intuitive level; the word of knowledge is the revelation of information which has not been rationally deduced. To use it I must act in the faith that what I have received is accurate and from God, open to the possibility of making a mistake. If I do not take the first risk I will never begin. The same principle can be applied to prophecy, healing, miracles, discernment and many other gifts. In each situation where we believe God may be prompting us to exercise a gift, we are to act in faith, taking the risk. God honours real faith and is well able to instruct us if we are wrong. Ministry is learned in the doing. God 'supplies the Spirit to you and works miracles among you by... hearing with faith' (Gal 3:5).

Whereas it is true that the gifts of the Spirit are not marks of maturity, it must be obvious that their mature use does require faith and Christian character. The training and testing which comes through our circumstances is as much training for ministry as for anything else. Often those who are most effective in ministering to others are those who have been brought to an end of themselves, who have come to a point of brokenness, through suffering and trials, and have themselves received ministry from God directly or through their fellow Christians. It is when we have been brought to the end of ourselves that we begin to rely on the power of God. It is when we have needed comfort ourselves that we become sensitive to the needs of others. Mature ministry requires a deep inner work of God. Paul's powerful ministry of the gifts of the Spirit had this foundation (2 Cor 1:3-11, Rom 15:18).

'Power without weakness is destructive, only *charismata* which manifest power in weakness build up the community (2 Cor 10:8, 13:10). This is clearly why Paul *never* boasts of his *charismata*, but rather of his weakness (11:30), for it is only when he is conscious of his own weakness, that is, when he is not seeking to manipulate or direct the power of God in any way - only then can God's grace and power fully rest upon him, and manifest itself through him (12:9).' [11]

The Church does not own the Holy Spirit. The Holy Spirit owns the Church. Openness to the Lord who is the Spirit is the basic prerequisite of Christian ministry.

Notes over the page

NOTES
Biblical quotations are from the Revised Standard Version.

1. Ronald Metcalfe *Sharing Christian Ministry* (Oxford: Mowbray, 1981), p 5
2. Robert Banks *Paul's Idea of Community* (Exeter: Paternoster, 1980), p 111
3. James Dunn *Jesus and the Spirit* (London: SCM 1975), p 202
4. James Dunn 'A Gift to Be Handled with Care' in *Towards Renewal* 19 (Autumn 1979),p4
5. Jürgen Moltmann*The Church in the Power of the Spirit* (London: SCM,1977), p 296-7
6. Charles Hummel *Fire in the Fireplace* (Oxford: Mowbray, 1979), p 185
7. Arnold Bittlinger *Gifts and Ministries* (Grand Rapids: Eerdmans, 1974), p 21
8. Howard Snyder *The Community of the King* (Downers Grove: IVP/USA, 1978), p 67
9. Jürgen Moltmann *The Open Church* (London: SCM, 1978), p 33
10. Dietrich Bonhoeffer *Life Together* (London: SCM 1972), p 15
11. James Dunn *Jesus and the Spirit* (London: SCM, 1975), p 329

RECOMMENDED READING

James Dunn *Jesus and the Spirit* (London: SCM,1975), part 3
Jürgen Moltmann *The Church in the Power of the Spirit* (London: SCM,1977), ch VI
Robert Banks *Paul's Idea of Community* (Exeter: Paternoster, 1980), chs 9-10

© Graham Cray 1985

This section was originally produced for St Michael-le-Belfrey Church, York, and is reproduced by kind permission.

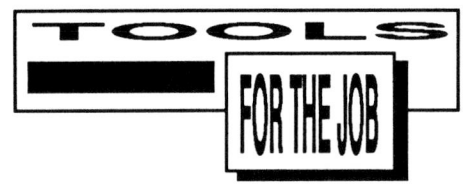

3. LEADERSHIP IN THE LOCAL CHURCH

Graham Cray

JESUS IS LORD

The controlling principle of local church leadership is that Jesus is the active leader of each congregation. As Lawrence Richards has written, 'The Church is a living organism with Jesus Christ himself functioning as head. In seeing Jesus as head, we must take seriously the notion that he is not head 'emeritus'. He is not some titular chairman of the board who is given nodding acknowledgement while others run his organisation, he is not the retired founder of the firm. God has appointed Jesus to be 'head over all things for the church which is the body.' Leaders are not in charge of churches, Jesus is. Richards continues, 'a living organism can have only one head, and the functions of the head can never be delegated to other parts of the body.' Jesus' leadership defines the limits and the purpose of our leadership and ministry.

EVERY MEMBER MINISTRY

Jesus exercises his leadership of the church by the gifts of the Spirit given to each believer. Ministry involves everyone (Eph 4:12). In the Bible's terms all are 'priests' and all are 'laypeople' (1 Pet 2:9). Our acceptance by Jesus is so complete that each conversion recruits the new believer for active service. All gifts and ministries are Christ's initiatives, by the Spirit, through the church. When healing is needed, Jesus takes the initiative with a gift of healing, and so with all the other gifts.

In this sense the authority for leadership at any particular moment lies with the one prompted to minister the required gift. In the most literal way Jesus is actively leading his church, involving all his servants as he does so. Our responsibility is to be open to his leading and initiatives. But if in one sense Jesus is the only leader, yet in another all are involved in his leadership, where do human leaders fit in?

THE PLACE AND PURPOSE OF LEADERSHIP

Leadership is a specific role of ministry within the body of Christ, not a special status. It is not a matter of controlling the people of God, but of equipping them (Eph 4:11, 12). Church is not the religious part of our lives, but the whole of all our lives in Christ. Leaders are not raised up to control the details of church members lives, but to equip them to live in obedience to Jesus in all that they do. All ministry has the same status, but leadership has the special role of serving the people of God so that they may all minister and co-ordinate their individual ministries to fufill a common vision. As such, there are three primary functions of local church leadership:

(a) To discern, encourage and order the gifts of church members.

If Jesus actively leads his local church by the gifts of the Spirit, then leaders have a vital role in helping each member to be open to the Spirit, to know how he has gifted them, to encourage and train them to use gifts wisely, maturely and in faith, and to order and structure the life of the church so as to free each one to make their contribution. (In conjunction with this, please see my other paper 'Ministry in the Local Church - The Gifts of the Spirit', especially the section on 'The Nurture and Recognition of Gifts'.) The chief task is to discern what Jesus is doing, or wants to do by the Spirit. Just as Jesus only did what he saw his Father doing (Jn 5:19) and only said what he heard from his Father (Jn 5:30) so we are sent by him

(Jn 20:21), endued by the Spirit as he was (Jn 1:32, 20:22) and are to discern and cooperate with what he is doing in his church. Initiatives of the Spirit do not always come through leaders, but leaders need the ability to discern what comes from God, from what does not. If Jesus delights to speak and act through all Christians (including leaders of course), then leaders must know how to recognise and respond to his initiatives.

(b) To model vision.

Because leaders are 'overseers' (Acts 20:28), called to care for the whole church, they have a special responsibility to discern their church's future direction and guiding vision, although they will listen to the Lord *in* his people as much as *for* his people. Then they are called to be the first to live out what they have received. To do this it is essential that the overall leadership of a congregation be shared. There is no biblical precedent for a one man (or woman) ministry.

When Jesus saw the crowds 'like sheep without a shepherd' his response was to appoint the twelve (Mt 9:35-10:4). Local church leadership in the New Testament is always in the plural. It is never a one man show (Acts 14:23, 20:17, Phil 1:1, Titus 1:5). Elders were appointed, not elected. (By Moses - Ex 18:13-27, Num 11:14-17; by Jesus - Mk 3:13-19; by Paul and Barnabas - Acts 14:23; by Timothy - 1 Tim 3:1-13; by Titus - Titus 1:5-9), but the congregation's discernment of leadership gifts was also important (Acts 6:3). Various patterns of shared leadership appear: Acts 15 - apostles and elders led by James: Acts 20 - elders answerable to Paul; 1 Tim & Titus - bishops and deacons led by Timothy or Titus; Acts 13 - prophets and teachers; Eph 4 - apostles, prophets, evangelists, pastors and teachers. The situation was clearly a flexible one, related to local needs and circumstances and the emergence of gifts. Archbishop Stuart Blanch has written, 'The ordering of the church, the authority of particular people within it and the organisation of the priesthood are essentially matters of contingency. They have no eternal quality, they are interim provisions for the people of God, as they wait for the coming of their Lord in glory.' Almost every leadership pattern currently in use in the different denominations can be traced to one or other 'proof text', and no group may claim that they exclusively have the truth. The point is not that we can justify our particular system from the New Testament, but that the New Testament directs us to be flexible. The Body of Christ is an organism not merely an organisation and its leadership is to be both shared and flexible to the leading of the Spirit in changing circumstances. In churches which traditionally have had a vicar or minister in sole overall charge, the best solution is for that minister to share his leadership with a team of elders.

Jesus called the twelve 'to be with him' (Mk 3:13), he was their undisputed leader and their authority was derived from his leadership (Mk 3:14-15). He opened his life to them and led them by example as well as teaching them. However, there is one vital difference between modern ministers and the Lord Jesus. We are sinners. It is therefore essential that a shared leadership should be a mutually submitted leadership. Each member, including any 'presiding elder' needs to have his life open and submitted to his fellows, for their encouragement and correction. This openness and depth of relationship is required of all Christians and must therefore be lived by the leadership. All leadership, including that of a 'presiding elder', is a calling to exercise a particular role in the Body of Christ, not to a different status. No leader may hide behind his status to avoid the correction he needs from his colleagues. Furthermore all leadership decisions need to be genuinely joint decisions, not forced through by a chairman or those with more assertive personalities.

Shared leadership has far more inbuilt safeguards than one man leadership, but it can still go wrong. Divisions can be created through the members of a church making wrong comparisons between different leaders (1 Cor 1:10-17, 3:1-23), or committing themselves to particular leaders for wrong motives (2 Tim 4:3). False teachers from outside can seem so much more 'spiritual' than a church's own leaders (2 Cor 11, Acts 20:29). Personal ambition can overcome an elder (Acts 20:30, 2 Tim 4:10).

Vision precedes the first establishment of leadership, which must be committed to that vision. Paul established his churches upon a certain understanding of the gospel which he had received (1 Cor 15:1-4) and which he had taken care to check out with those who were in Christ before him (Gal 1:11-2:10). He appointed elders to continue in that tradition, to protect each local church from being led astray (Acts 20:17-38), and to pass on the vision to the next generation (2 Tim 2:1-2).

The heart of this vision is found in the nature of God himself, revealed in the gospel as Father, Son and Holy Spirit. Out of this comes an understanding of the nature of the Body of Christ, its unity and relationships. The Lord God has revealed himself as three persons in total self-giving love. God is community. The triune God reaches out to save fallen people and to include them into his fellowship. Churches are called to be such communities and leaders are called to demonstrate what that means in their context. Following the model revealed in the Trinity, 'I am free and feel myself to be free when I am recognised and accepted by others and when I, for my part, recognise and accept others. I become truly free when I open my life for others and share it with them, and when others open their lives for me and share their lives with me. Then the other person is no longer a limitation on my freedom but the completion of it' (Jürgen Moltmann). Leaders need to live this with one another and in their attitude to those they lead.

Large parts of the epistles are written to correct and maintain the quality of corporate life and relationship of the different churches. In other words, vision is an understanding of the nature of the church and its mission in the light of the gospel and as applied to a specific local situation. It concerns the fundamental nature of the church and its mission, rather than the specific emphasis or directions of the Spirit of God to that church at any particular moment. This does not mean that it is an entirely static thing, but that all innovations, changes of emphasis or tradition need to be checked against it. It concerns the nature of a church's spirituality. Renewal comes to a long-standing church through renewed understanding of the corporate implications of the gospel, thus vision is re-established on the basis of the New Testament and each elder in a shared leadership needs to give himself without reserve to that understanding.

In churches where eldership is revised or re-appointed at regular intervals, it may fall to the minister or presiding elder to safeguard that vision in the long term. The object however, is not to have a body of elders who are willing to 'put up with' the vision for the sake of a share in the responsibility, rather, as Tom Lees writes, 'Corporate leaders have taken to themselves the individual vision and have made it part of themselves. They have laid aside their own ideas, prejudices and desires and have fully grasped the vision. They have no more investment of their own. They have died to themselves and have committed themselves totally to the vision at the cost of their own lives and convenience.' Such a vision establishes the basic unalterable minimum of a church's self understanding in the light of the Scriptures. It provides the fixed point which frees a leadership to respond flexibly and safely to each new situation. It gives the basis for long term planning and decreases the proportion of necessary crisis management. Any church which sets out to answer the question 'What do we do?', or even 'What is God saying to us now?', without having first consciously answered the question 'What are we?', is heading into difficulties, a loss of sense of direction, and possible division.

(c) To exercise discipline on behalf of the whole congregation

It is quite clear from the New Testament that leaders in a local church are to have authority over those in their Church ('over you and admonish you' [1 Thess 5:12], 'elders who rule well' [1 Tim 5:17], 'be subject to such men' [1 Cor 16:16], 'overseers' [Acts 20:28], 'obey your leaders and submit to them' [Heb 13:17], 'in your charge', 'be subject to the elders' [1 Pet 5:2,5]). Equally clearly the discipline and restoration of those guilty of serious lapses into sin is a matter of concern for the whole church (Mt 18:15-17, 1 Cor 5:1-5, 2 Cor 1:23-2:11, Gal 6:1-6). Leaders exercise authority on behalf of the body.

It is essential to understand how that authority is acquired and how it is to be exercised. We should expect Christian leadership and authority to be of a different order to their secular counterparts. 'You know that those who are supposed to rule over the Gentiles lord it over them, and their great men exercise authority over them. *But it shall not be so among you;* but whoever would be great among you must be your servant, and whoever would be first among you must be slave of all' (Mark 10:42-44).

The distinctive Christian words for leadership are 'servant', 'service' or 'slave'. Our English titles 'minister' and 'deacon' come directly from the Latin and Greek words for servant. The New Testament leadership titles and terms imply an attitude of heart much more than an official position (eg 1 Tim 3:8 'deacons', 4:6 'minister', and 1:12 'service' all use the same Greek word for service). The origin of all this is found in the teaching and example of the Lord Jesus: 'for the Son of Man also came not to be served, but to serve, and to give his life as a ransom for many' (Mark 10:45).

In other words the Christian leader has to choose between two types of authority, only one of which is true to the gospel. Either he imposes his authority, on the basis of his alleged 'status' as a leader ('lord it' [Mark 10:42], 'domineering' [1 Pet 5:3]), or he is given effective authority by those he leads, on the basis of his example and evident willingness to lay his life down for them. Jesus had to make this claim. Imposed authority was offered to him by the devil (Lk 4:6) but the temptation was refused. However, the disciples and the crowds willingly gave Jesus authority (Mt 7:28-29). The distinction between 'imposed' and 'given' authority is not to say that the Christian leader does not have a right to exercise discipline in situations of heretical teaching or gross immorality, whether or not the offending person recognises his authority. Rather it is to say that changes in behaviour in a congregation have to be made willingly, and that there is far greater scope for willing changes in response to leadership which is trusted, because the leaders set an example and are willing to make costly sacrifices for those they lead. The only effective Christian leadership is 'servant' leadership.

GOD'S EQUIPMENT FOR LEADERSHIP

God's equipment for ministry is the Holy Spirit himself. He makes us competent 'to be ministers of a new covenant in the Spirit' (2 Cor 3:4-6). All of our ministry needs to be in the power of the Spirit (1 Cor 2:1-5). However, the Spirit equips us in three distinct ways.

(a) **God's Call**. Each leader must know that he is called by God to lead (Acts 13:2, 1 Tim 1:18). During times of struggle or frustration it is the only thing which keeps us going. For a Christian 'the bottom line' is not his ability or his 'results', but the call of God.

(b) **God's Gifts**. If every Christian is to minister on the basis of the gifts distributed to him or her by the Spirit (1 Cor 12:11), leaders cannot be exempt. We are to fulfill the vision of leadership outlined in this paper by exercising the gifts we have, and seeking those which God shows us he wishes to give us, not by being 'one man bands'. There needs to be an interdependence of ministries and complementary gifts within a leadership team. The gifts are the tools for the job. God is not like Pharaoh - demanding that we make bricks *and* find our own straw (Exod 5). But we are to exercise the gifts we have, not the ones we wish we had. Timothy had gifts of evangelism and teaching and was tempted to undervalue, and not use them (1 Tim 4:11-16, 2 Tim 1:6, 4:1-5). Whatever gifts God has given us, we are to use them and not try to minister where we are not gifted.

(c) **Our Example.** The gifts of the Spirit and the fruit of the Spirit are inseparable. People copy what we are, as individuals and together, rather than automatically do what we say. The New Testament places great emphasis on the authority of example (Acts 20:17-35, 1 Thess 1:4-7, 1 Tim 4:11-16, 2 Tim 3:10, Heb 13:7, 1 Pet 5:2-3, etc). Earlier we spoke of Christian leadership as servant leadership. What then are the characteristics of servant leaders?

1   Under Christ's Authority

A servant leader must be under Christ's authority, just as he was under his Father's authority. The centurion believed that Jesus had authority to heal his servant because he also was 'a man under authority' (Mt 8:8-9). Jesus constantly repeated that he did not act on his own authority. 'I can do nothing on my own authority; as I hear I judge and my judgement is just, because I seek not my own will but the will of him who sent me' (Jn 5:30). Jesus had effective and not just theoretical authority because of this, and his willingness to lay down his life for those he led. In the same way, he grants his authority to those he calls to be his leaders, 'as the Father has sent me, so I send you' (Jn 20:21). The authority he gives is the authority to serve, not dominate. 'What we preach is not ourselves, but Jesus Christ as Lord, with ourselves as your servants for Jesus sake' (2 Cor 4:5).

2   Living a Consistent Life

The Christian leader's authority comes through the power of example, (1 Pet 5:3, 1 Cor 4:16, 11:1, Phil 4:9, 1 Tim 4:12, Heb 6:12, 13:7, 1 Thess 1:6-7). He is not to be like the Pharisees, of whom Jesus said, 'practise and observe whatever they tell you, but not what they do' (Mt 23:3). Thus Archbishop Runcie has said, 'Even when we speak, as we must, the life-giving truths in the precious words of Scripture handed down to us, those words can lack authority because what we are will deny what we say.....For the Church to have the authority of Jesus, it must live now as Jesus Christ would live now.' There must be no 'playing the part' of a servant, or acting a role. Paul tells us that we are to have the mind of Christ who was in 'the form of God' and took 'the form of a servant' (Phil 2:5-7). 'In the Kingdom of God service is not a stepping stone to nobility, it is nobility, the only kind of nobility that is recognised' (T W Manson).

3   Unconcerned about Personal Status or Reputation

Jesus never sought his own glory and was not concerned to defend his own reputation. 'He who speaks on his own authority, seeks his own glory, but he who seeks the glory of him who sent him is true and in him there is no falsehood' (Jn 7:18). The consequence was that the crowds 'glorified God, who had given such authority to men' (Mt 9:8). It was Satan who offered authority with glory (Lk 4:6). Jesus gave up his rights to be a servant (Phil 2:5-8, Jn 13:3-5). When he said that the Son of Man came 'not to be served but to serve' he would have astounded his hearers who read of the Son of Man, 'to him was given dominion, and glory and kingdom, that all peoples, nations and languages should *serve him*' (Dan 7:14). As models for greatness in God's kingdom Jesus chose the slave (Mk 10:44), the child (Mk 9:33f) and the youngest (Lk 22:26). Such an attitude is typified by the pastor in the book *The Jesus Family in Communist China* (by D.V. Rees [Exeter, Paternoster, 1973]), who explained that since they were all equal, he, the leader, had the privilege of doing the worst jobs. Christian leadership has no special status, for there is no higher status than that of a child of the living God. It is a call to share the servanthood of Jesus.

4   No Desire to Control or Manipulate Others

Jesus went to the cross willingly 'for the joy that was set before him'. His Father did not manipulate or force him. In the same way Christian leaders are not to be domineering, but examples (1 Pet 5:3). The Gospel levels all hierarchies, all are brothers and sisters and there is no greater privilege. All, leaders included, are to live in mutual submission and humility (1 Pet 5:5). All are servants of the others, and the servant has no power or authority other than that of a layed down life, and the trust that results. There can be no 'lording it'. Those who would appear to be leaders in family life, husbands, parents and masters of slaves, are to exercise their 'headship' by sacrificial love and giving themselves up. The Christian leader is to set his people an example in this way of relating. He goes still lower to help all his brothers live this way, 'ourselves as your servants for Christ's sake' (2 Cor 4:5). If there is any hierarchy it is:

JESUS
CHURCH MEMBERS
ELDERS

Not that the ordinary believers have authority over the elders, who are answerable to Christ ('Jesus Christ as Lord' [2 Cor 4:5]), but the elders earn their authority over their brethren by the quality of their service. Correction will sometimes need to be given, but changes in lifestyles cannot be forced on others. Rather we correct gently, without manipulation, trusting God to grant repentance (2 Tim 2:24-26).

5 Gentleness

The mark of servant leadership is gentleness. Jesus proclaimed his authority with the words, 'all things have been delivered to me by my Father', but went on to say, 'Come unto me.....for I am gentle.' (Mt 11:27-30) In the same way Christian leaders are to use Christ's authority with gentleness. 'I, Paul, myself entreat you by the meekness and gentleness of Christ.' (2 Cor 10:1). 'The Lord's servant must be kindly to everyone... correcting his opponents with gentleness' (2 Tim 2:24-25). The same principle is applied to the care of new believers, 'we were gentle among you, like a nurse taking care of her children' (1 Thess 2:7), and to the restoration of Christians who fall into sin: 'If a man is overtaken in any trespass you who are spiritual should restore him in a spirit of gentleness' (Gal 6:1). At the heart of this principle is a concern not to place unreasonable burdens on those we serve. Jesus offered his yoke as a remedy for the 'heavy laden'. Paul was gentle with the Thessalonians, and 'worked night and day, that we might not burden any of you'. The restoration of those who sin is part of the principle 'bear one another's burdens'. By contrast the Pharisees 'bind heavy burdens hard to bear and lay them on men's shoulders; but they themselves will not move them with their finger' (Mt 23:4). In other words we are not to make demands on those we lead which we would not make on ourselves, or which we are not willing to share with them. This concern to be gentle must be kept especially in mind when church programmes are being planned. It is quite possible to be gentle in personal pastoral ministry, while at the same time being quite brutal in the demands we make on our people to attend meetings and take responsibility. A recent survey showed that the demands of the local church were the chief cause of stress in the first five years of Christian marriage.

6 Open about Personal Weakness

Jesus was open about his inner life with those to whom he lived the closest. 'My soul is very sorrowful even to death' (Mk 14:34). 'Jesus wept' (Jn 11:35). 'Now is my soul troubled' (Jn 12:27). A disciple who had been one of his closest companions for three years could write, 'He committed no sin, no guile was found on his lips' (1 Pet 2:22). Our lives need to be as transparent to those whom we lead: but for us that will mean the acknowledgement of our own sin and weakness. That is not to suggest that we reveal all our personal sins to young believers, but we do have to be honest and open about our personal weakness and inner conflicts. Gene Beerens writes, 'It is difficult to believe that the unveiling of personal weakness will be life giving, but that is one of the things that makes us approachable and accountable and credible as servant leaders.' We should not fear that our people will lose respect for us if we let them see that we are as they are. A great part of 2 Corinthians is written to show that Paul's authority as an apostle was based on the power of God in his weakness. Paul also willingly shared his heart with those in his care (eg 2 Cor 1:8, 2:4, 12:7-9).

7 A Life Lived for Others, Whatever the Cost

To sum up: servant leadership is leadership which follows the example of Jesus who 'having loved his own who were in the world, loved them to the uttermost' (Jn 13:1), even to the point of laying down his life. It was through giving his life for us that he gained his rightful authority over us. We now love him, because he first loved us (1 Jn 4:10). It was through his obedience to death, that he gained the name at which every knee shall bow. Our limited authority is gained in the same way. 'If you will be a servant to this people, and serve them.....then they will be your servants for ever.'(1 Kings 12:7). We shall only share Christ's authority so that our ministry causes others to willingly change their lives, when we lead as he led. 'It matters desperately how the church seeks to exercise authority. Aggression and compulsion was not the way of Jesus Christ, who came among us in the form of a servant and shared our suffering... this deep love has in itself an authority which makes people question and change the way in which they are living' (Archbishop Runcie).

8 Refuses to Exploit the Authority Given by Others

All the preceding points (i-viii) are the basis of Christian ('given') authority; but Jesus did not only resist the temptation to take ('imposed') authority wrongly (Lk 4:5-8); he also refused to let the crowds give him too much authority (Jn 6:15). There are strict limits to the authority of any Christian leader. We are all brothers and sisters, with no hierarchy. We share in the priesthood of all believers, each having access to the Father, through Jesus the one mediator between God and man. Leaders have authority over doctrine and morality among their own people, as defined by the Bible, but there is little evidence of either Jesus or the apostles giving their followers personal directions about the details of their lives. There is no scriptural basis for the idea that each believer must have a 'shepherd' to disciple him. Never be the Holy Spirit for someone else. Never take responsibility for another's life which is theirs before God alone. Rather, be his servant to help him act responsibly before God and to live in interdependence with his fellow believers. We are to 'bear one another's burdens', because 'each man will have to bear his own load' (Gal 6:2,5).

LEADERSHIP AND GROWTH

Growth to maturity in the Body of Christ, both individually and corporately, depends upon two things: the quality of relationships between believers, and the ministry of each member (Eph 4:11-16). Robert Banks writes of the New Testament Church, 'the focal point of reference was neither a book nor a rite but a *set of relationships*, and God communicated himself through one another.' (in *Paul's Idea of Community* [Exeter: Paternoster, 1980], p111).

The role of leadership is first, to demonstrate that quality of relationships between themselves; to embody the vision, and to motivate others towards it. Second, it is to use their gifts to equip each one to contribute to the building up of the Body. Growth does not come through the relationship of each Christian to a leader, but through the depth of their relationships to each other under Christ, and the use of the gifts which emerge in that quality of love. Leadership, including individual pastoral care, is to build that quality of shared life, to make growth possible.

Recommended Reading over the page.

RECOMMENDED READING

Lawrence Richards & Clyde Hoeldthe
A Theology of Church Leadership
(Grand Rapids: Zondervan, 1980)
Written for an American context, expensive, but the main text is excellent.

Paul Miller
Leading the Family of God
(Scottdale: Herald Press, 1981)

Philip Greenslade
Leadership
(Basingstoke: Marshalls, 1984)
The best of the 'House Church' material on leadership - good, but to be read with discernment.

Henri Nouwen, McNeill and Morrison
Compassion
(London: DLT,1982)
Superb on the nature of servanthood.

Elisabeth and Jürgen Moltmann
Humanity in God
(London: SCM, 1984)
A patchy book, but Jürgen in chs 4-6 is brilliant on the Trinity as a basis for vision.

Jean Vanier
Community and Growth
(London: DLT, 1979)
Community and the place of 'gifts' and leadership in it: very wise.

© Graham Cray 1985

This section was originally produced for St Michael-le-Belfrey Church, York, and is reproduced by kind permission.

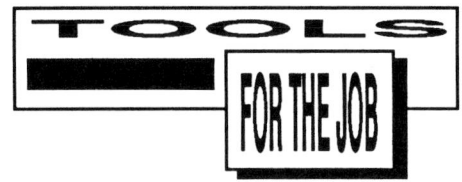

4. SPIRITUAL GIFTS AND PERSONAL MINISTRY

Graham Cray

These notes apply the New Testament teaching on the gifts of the Holy Spirit to personal ministry, whether in an evangelistic or pastoral context. They act as a supplement to Section 3 'Ministry in the Local Church - The Gifts of the Spirit'.

MAKING THE INVISIBLE VISIBLE

The Lord Jesus is the full and perfect expression of God in human form (Jn 1:18, Col 2:9). He is no longer physically visible. (1 Pet 1:8, Jn 20:29). The purpose of the church on earth is to give a mature expression of Jesus in each generation and place, in character and action. (Each place - Eph 1:23; Each generation - Eph 3:21; Mature corporate expression - Eph 4:12-13; Action - Eph 2:10, 4:12.)

Through the church, the realities of the 'heavenly realms' are to be made visible. 'Heavenly realms' = 'the unseen world of spiritual reality' John Stott *The Message of Ephesians* (Leicester: IVP, 1979), p 273 (Eph 1:3,20, 2:6, 3:10, 6:12).

The Kingdom of God, which began on earth through the Lord Jesus is also called the Kingdom of Heaven (Matthew's Gospel). 'Your kingdom come, your will be done on earth as it is in heaven' (Mt 6:10).

The reality of God's power: Eph 1:3,19, 3:20.
The reality of the enemy: Eph 3:10, 5:11, 6:12.
The reality of Christ's victory: Eph 1:20-22, 6:10-20.

All this is achieved through the Holy Spirit: 'Keep on letting the Holy Spirit fill you' (Eph 5:18). This is an experience (as is getting drunk, but alcohol is a depressant, the Holy Spirit is a stimulant.) It is repeatable, not a permanent state. We are required to be open to the sovereign operation of the Spirit. Our greatest need is to 'see' the invisible spiritual realities we are to minister (Eph 1:17-22).

JESUS - OUR MODEL FOR MINISTRY

Jesus fulfilled his ministry as a man in the power of God.(Acts 2:22, 10:38). He has commissioned us to exercise a ministry patterned on his ministry (Jn 14:12, 20:21).

Jesus had no power in himself (Jn 5:19). Nor do we (Jn 15:5).
Jesus needed revelation (Jn 5:19-32: NB 'see' v 19; 'hear' v 30).
He was totally committed to the Father's will (Jn 5:30).
His words came from the Father (Jn 7:16-18, 28-30).
His actions came by direction from the Father (Jn 5:19).
He was trusted by the Father to act and speak for the Father (Jn 5:22).
His ministry arose from his intimate relationship with the Father (Jn 11:41-44). So will ours (Jn 15, 17).
All he needed for ministry, he received by faith (Jn 5:37-38, Jn 6:28-29, Jn 14:12-14).

GIFTS OF THE SPIRIT

The gifts of the Holy Spirit are the outworking of the Spirit-filled life (Eph 5:18) as applied to specific situations. They are the 'manifestation of the Spirit' (1 Cor 12:7). The Holy Spirit is the invisible representative of the invisible Lord Jesus (1 Cor 12:7). He is made visible through what he does 'There are certain kinds of action and utterance which demonstrate the Spirit's presence and activity.' [James Dunn] The gifts are continually given, on the basis of each situation's need, according to the Holy Spirit's sovereign decision.(1 Cor 12:7,11). Each believer is to be open to the whole range of the Spirit's activity.

The ministry of spiritual gifts is specific and clear-cut, however it is not unambiguous to unbelievers or Christians who have not been instructed in this dimension of ministry (1 Cor 12:7, 2 Cor 4:2, 1 Cor 2:10-3:1, 14:23- 25).

These gifts are available for pastoral ministry (1 Cor 12-14) and for evangelism (1 Cor 14:24-25, Heb 2:3-4, plus the many evangelistic encounters in the Gospels and Acts - eg Jn 4, Acts 8).

Co-operation with the Spirit

God does not bypass your humanity, but uses it. A spiritual gift is 'a gracious manifestation of the Holy Spirit, working in and through, but going beyond the believer's natural ability.' [Arnold Bittlinger] Gifts are received by faith in the intuitive realm, not logically deduced. They are sometimes experienced physically. (See *Come Holy Spirit* by David Pytches for details relating to each gift.)

Danger Points

(a) Mistaking your wisdom, knowledge and experience for God's revelation. Prayer ministry is not counselling, although each is important in its own context, and each involves drawing from established experience and openness to the Spirit's insight for the occasion (Mt 13:52).

(b) Pride. Spiritual gifts are not marks of maturity (1 Cor 1:4-7, 3:1). They are manifestations of grace, ie undeserved (1 Cor 1:4, 4:7). They provide no basis for pride.(1 Cor 4:8, 8:1-3). Our ministry of gifts will be imperfect until Jesus' coming makes them unnecessary (1 Cor 13:9-10).

FOR FURTHER STUDY

John Wimber
Power Evangelism
(Hodder & Stoughton)

David Pytches
Come Holy Spirit
(Hodder & Stoughton)

George Mallone, ed
Those Controversial Gifts
(Hodder & Stoughton)

Charles Hummel
Fire in the Fireplace
(Mowbrays)

Michael Green
I Believe in the Holy Spirit
(Hodder & Stoughton)

© Graham Cray 1987

This section was originally produced for St Michael- le-Belfrey Church, York, and is reproduced by kind permission.

5. THE GIFTS OF THE SPIRIT IN THE LOCAL CHURCH

Derek Little

1 WHAT THE GIFTS ARE

Called to Serve

Every Christian is called by God; we would not be God's people unless called by him. This calling involves being called to serve (see Eph 4:12). As Michael Green has written, 'The New Testament gives no suggestion that one could possibly be a Christian without at the same time being called to some ministry within the church.' (1)

The attitude we are to have is the one of Jesus, who came to serve, not to be served (Phil 2:5-7, Mark 10:45). Dietrich Bonhoeffer has written, 'The church does not need brilliant personalities but faithful servants of Jesus and the brethren. Not in the former but in the latter is the lack.' (2)

Equipped by God

Just as God calls us to serve, he equips us to do so by his Holy Spirit. He does not call us to a particular form of service without equipping us to do it. 'In the New Testament the words *'minister'* and *'ministry'* apply not so much to a position, status, job description or pattern of activity as to an inner desire to serve, empowered and led by the Spirit, in response to Christ's call.' (3)

Ministry/service, like every aspect of the Christian life, is an experience of the grace (charis) of God. 'In the New Testament grace is not a theoretical doctrine, but is always in action and experience...The charisma of God is eternal life itself, and the gifts of the Spirit are specific manifestations of that life to uphold and upbuild the local church.' (3)

We are to expect to see evidence of the Spirit's 'gifting for service' in every believer. See, for example, 1 Cor 12:7, where Paul writes about the Spirit's presence being 'shown in each person' (GNB); the context here is one of service. So, the gifts of the Spirit are **tools for the job**, the job being 'Service to the church and to the world.'

The Gifts of the Spirit

The gifts can be used to benefit us personally, for example the private use of tongues. In this paper, however, we are concerned with their primary use which is within, and on behalf of, the body of Christ.

The source is from the Father and the Son by the Spirit (1 Cor 12:4-6). We cannot have the gifts without the Giver; neither should we regard being filled with the Spirit as an end in itself. As Graham Cray says, 'To be asked to be filled with the Holy Spirit without being willing to minister spiritual gifts is a *non sequitur*.' (3)

The context is that of the Christian life as a shared life. Spiritual gifts are not given to individual Christians in isolation or merely to have a 'spiritual whoopee'; they are given to the church, being exercised by individual members of the church. The New Testament gives an overall picture of the corporate life in Christ shared by God's people.

What are the Gifts for?

They are acts of God's power (see Eph 3:7). "When there is a genuine gift of the Holy Spirit something happens. The gifts are not personal emotional experiences; they are acts of God's power achieving his purposes.' (3) If someone is exercising a spiritual gift we should expect to see results.

There are varieties of gifts. This variety is clearly seen as we read through the four main passages in the New Testament which refer to the gifts of the Spirit, i.e. 1 Cor 12, Rom 12, Eph 4, 1 Pet 4. These are not exhaustive lists. God is the giver and he can work in countless ways, so we cannot number or restrict his gifts. There is also a sense in which gifts overlap each other. 'Sometimes the gifts are described in terms of function (e.g. healing); sometimes the person through whom the function is ministered is called the gift (e.g. teacher). Rather than being in watertight compartments, the various gifts merge into one another like colours of the rainbow.' (3)

Because there is a wide variety of gifts, distributed by God as he wills (see Eph 4:7) there is no need to envy others' gifts or despise our own. No Christian has all the gifts, and we all need our ministries complemented by those of others so that 'the whole body grows and builds itself up through love' (Eph 4:16).

Spiritual gifts and natural talents. It is interesting to see how two people who approach the subject from different 'positions' agree that there need not be an either/ or situation here. In his book *Serving Grace* Michael Griffiths writes, 'We cannot drive a wedge between natural gifts and spiritual gifts - God our Creator is not a different person from God our Redeemer. There is every reason why the sovereign God should give to his servants in their mother's wombs natural abilities which, when surrendered, tempered and transfigured by God's grace may be effectively used for God's glory.' (4) Graham Cray states, 'The distinction between 'natural' and 'supernatural' is not a biblical one. Each gift involves the 'natural' and 'supernatural'. Our natural abilities only become gifts of the Spirit under the specific calling and anointing of God. Similarly the apparently more supernatural gifts involve thoroughly human activity.' (3)

Gifts and Ministries (One-off and long-term). The primary emphasis in the New Testament is that all Christians are to be open to any gifting from God at any time. 1 Cor 12:7 gives us a picture of the Holy Spirit moving among the people of God giving different gifts as he wills. These are not the possession of each person, but are freely given by the Spirit for a specific purpose. Having said that it is important to note also that the Spirit gives particular long- term gifts to different Christians. 'The Spirit distributes gifts according to the needs and opportunities of the Body of Christ. However the New Testament is clear that each Christian has been given a specific gift or gifts, that he is to know what it is and to use it. It may be easier to speak of a 'ministry' when referring to the consistent long term use of a specific gift, and 'gift' to refer to each specific occurrence.' (3)

2 FINDING OUR GIFTS AND MINISTRIES

The context of our discovering these is obviously the church, in particular:

A church with teaching and pastoral care

The teaching ministry is of great importance in the life of the church. We need to be concerned about the whole of Christian doctrine as it is too easy to emphasise one facet of truth to the point where other biblical emphases are excluded. Included in this aspect of the church's ministry should be regular teaching about the gifts of the Spirit. 'Ministry will not develop if it is not taught. We only expect from God what we see promised in the Bible. Teaching instructs and builds faith to receive.' (3)

Teaching the congregation needs to be backed up with personal pastoral care. This will necessitate developing an effective pastoral oversight in the church - one person cannot effectively pastor a whole congregation.

A church with meaningful fellowship

Gifts are exercised by individuals but 'they are gifts to the body of Christ, gifts to an interdependent community. They need the setting of intimate fellowship both to emerge and mature. It is the responsibility of leaders to encourage that fellowship.' (3)

When a potential gift is discerned it will be helped to develop by linking the person concerned with someone already exercising the gift. This fosters encouragement and confidence.

Home groups are important in the development of gifts and ministries. In the group it is possible for fellowship to be more 'meaningful' as people relate on a more personal and intimate level. If our groups are regarded as places of Bible study and prayer only we need to look again at their role and enlarge it, so they can be places where gifts are encouraged, developed and exercised.

A church with commitment and love

For mutual interdependent ministry to be functioning Christians need to be deeply committed to each other. Love is the context in which the gifts of the Spirit flourish. Jesus is our model (see John 13:34) and loving as he loved involves total commitment. Just as he risked rejection, so must we; just as he forgave others freely, so must we. We are to take initiatives in restoring a broken relationship; we are to serve each other in practical ways; we are to be open to one another. 'We have to reach the point in our relationships where we *have* to rely on the Holy Spirit, where what each of us is is fully known, yet we are still loved, accepted, forgiven and trusted. In context of such love gifts blossom and there we mature in their use, for we are not afraid to speak and act in God's name in each other's company.' (3)

3 A WAY FORWARD

This is based on Peter Wagner's book Your Spiritual Gifts can Help Your Church Grow [MARC Europe]. You won't find the following headings in the book, but much of what is contained in this section is found in the book)

(a) **Look Up** - in prayer. Gifts are given to individuals and so it is the responsibility of each church member to receive, understand and use the gifts given by the Holy Spirit. We come to God in prayer, open to whatever he wants to give us and however he wants to use us. Ask someone to pray for you, perhaps with the laying on of hands.

(b) **Look In** - to the Bible to see what's on offer (e.g. the 'lists' in Romans 12; 1 Corinthians 12; Ephesians 4 and 1 Peter 4). Find out all you can about the gifts of the Spirit: read books on the subject and make it a talking point in your fellowship. Look in also to yourself and examine your feelings. 'God knows that if we enjoy doing a task we do a better job at it than if we do not enjoy it.' (5) A desire to do something may well be from God.

(c) **Look Out** - to others. Often others can see in us what we ourselves cannot see. Church leaders in particular have an important role here. It needs to be said that, 'If you think you have a spiritual gift and are trying to exercise it, but no-one else in your church thinks you have it - you probably don't.' (5) Gifts are exercised by individuals, but are given to the church, so they need to be confirmed by the Body.

(d) **Look Around** - and see what needs you can identify, then try to do something to meet a need. 'When true gifts are in operation, whatever is supposed to happen will happen.' (5) If, however, in experimenting with a gift you find that what it is supposed to do does not happen, you have probably discovered another gift God hasn't given you.

In exercising spiritual gifts we have to exercise faith. Faith is spelt R-I-S-K, and means being open to the possibility of making a mistake. God knows real faith and is well able to instruct us if we are wrong.

'The church does not own the Holy Spirit. The Holy Spirit owns the church. Openness to the Lord who is the Spirit is the basic prerequisite of Christian ministry.' (3)

4 WHAT ABOUT THE CLERGY?

With people exercising gifts and being involved in shared ministry, does this mean clergy are being phased out? Far from it. They have a vital role in the life of the church, which involves the following:

(a) **To lead.** 'Every member ministry' does not mean spiritual and ecclesiastical anarchy or democracy. The leadership role of clergy, properly exercised, is arguably more important than ever when spiritual gifts are in operation. Each minister must work out his or her style of leadership for each situation; whatever this is to be, leadership is not about ruling but serving.

(b) **To co-ordinate.** As has already been stressed, gifts are given to the church, to be used in the church and the community. The use of them needs co-ordination, encouraging and, where necessary, restraining. Christians are not to just 'do their own thing' in their own way; rather, gifts need to be co-ordinated in order for the church's ministry to be most effective. 'Gifts are not infallible utterances or unerring actions, and should operate in the context of the local church with its disciplines and safeguards. Those who manifest the gifts must always be in submission to others in the local church.' (6)

(c) **To enable.** This is the purpose of the leadership gifts referred to in Ephesians 4:11-12: 'to prepare all God's people for works of service.' (GNB) The minister has a responsibility to ensure that the necessary means are provided for people to develop and exercise their gifts and ministries. This is done in a variety of ways, including teaching; creating structures which facilitate the discovery of gifts and ministries; creating opportunities for people to test out their gifts; and encouraging openness to being 'gifted' by God any time in any situation.

'Spiritual gifts develop in the local church through teaching, which instructs the understanding and builds faith to appropriate what God offers, through the building up of the environment of fellowship in which they flourish, and through the initiative and action of leaders in recognising and 'imparting' gifts.' (3)

Quotations have been taken from the following publications:-

(1) Michael Green *Freed to Serve* (Hodder & Stoughton)
(2) Dietrich Bonhoeffer *Life Together* (SCM Press)
(3) 'Ministry in the local church - the Gifts of the Spirit'. (pages 39-48)
(4) Michael Griffiths *Serving Grace* (MARC)
(5) C Peter Wagner *Your Spiritual Gifts Can Help Your Church Grow* (MARC Europe)
(6) 'Spiritual gifts': a *Renewal* magazine study outline by Michael Harper - 1975

6. GOING ON FROM HERE

A   One church designed a form listing all the areas for service in the church and local community. The form was introduced in this way:

> **Following the course 'Tools for the Job', this church believes:**
>
> - All Christians are gifted.
> - Gifts are for service, not status.
> - Gifts are for building up the Church, the Body of Christ.
> - Gifts are not just for the Church, but for the world.
> - Each member should ask:-'Dare I take the risk of beginning/stepping out in faith?'
>
> The following opportunities for service exist at this very moment in our church/community. We urge you to take seriously the opportunities and see if there is something here for you. If there is, go ahead and contact the organiser mentioned. Your Homegroup leader or one of the clergy will be happy to discuss it with you.
>
> Maybe nothing strikes you - then talk to your Homegroup leader or one of the clergy about your gift and its use. Maybe for some it will be a matter of relinquishing a present job in order to take on another.
>
> OPPORTUNITIES FOR SERVICE IN OUR CHURCH/COMMUNITY

B   Another church has an annual 'Gifts in Action' questionnaire which all members are encouraged to complete. This lists a whole range of tasks which need doing and members are asked to commit themselves for one year. The tasks are divided into sections, e.g. administration/service/leadership/teaching and each section has a co-ordinator who seeks to use people wisely. This can be a major undertaking and there will be people who select inappropriate tasks.

Administry has produced resource papers on putting every member ministry into practice - including many pitfalls along the way. Recommended papers are 84.6 and 86.2. Contact : *Administry, 69 Sandridge Road, St Albans, Herts, AL1 4AG*

C   There are other questionnaires which people fill in, the results are analysed and people's major gifts are highlighted. For example the Wagner-Modified Houts Questionnaire asks 125 questions. Not for the faint-hearted. Available from *Charles E Fuller Institute, P.O. Box 91990, Pasadena, CA. 91109-1900, U.S.A.*

D   Any process involves doing the following in an organized way:
1. see each member as a person with unique gifts and abilities
2. enable members to see themselves in this way
3. consider tasks to be done and the spiritual gifts and personal qualities required
4. channel members into appropriate areas of service

A possible way forward is outlined below. The **LEADERSHIP TEAM** should:

1. Educate members on spiritual gifts. This is vital if members are to be motivated for gift-based ministry. A course like 'Tools for the Job' is really essential training ground and may have to be repeated to incorporate new members. Make good use of those with teaching gifts.

2. Conduct an interview with each member to help people discover their gifts and preferred areas of service. Ideally every member should go through this process for you are trying not just to recruit additional workers, but to help all your members invest their time and energy wisely.

   The result may be that some members who are 'stuck' in jobs for which they are unsuited are then released into new areas of service. Interviewers must be sensitive people who are able to draw people out and help them clarify their thoughts and feelings.

   The sort of questions to be asked at the interview are:

   a. In what ways have you served Christ both inside and outside the Christian community in the last 2 years?
   b. For each of these areas of service, have you
      i. found personal enjoyment
      ii. been successful
      iii. been accepted by others?
   c. Of all the areas of service, which did you enjoy most? Why?
   d. What do you now believe your spiritual gifts are?
   e. How do you think your spiritual gifts can best be employed in the Lord's service?

   The interviewee should be allowed to make any further comment which he/she thinks appropriate.

   Be aware of the diversity of spiritual gifts. They are not all for the activist. For example, someone who is shut-in may well be given the gift of being able to listen to God.

3. Make a list of all the positions in your church/community that need filling.

   A simple form of 'Job Description' is recommended. This should state:
   i. exactly what the tasks involve
   ii. how many hours will be involved
   iii. how long the job will last
   iv. gifts and skills required

   Some churches put up such a 'Job Description' on a 'Positions Vacant' board.

4. Allocate people to different tasks/areas of service/ministries. Those with the gift of administration are needed here. They will have to hold the system together and keep it running smoothly, handle details, keep records and make sure no one is left out.

> **Please be gracious and patient as you seek to develop a gift-based ministry.** Undergird everything with prayer. Before you can initiate change you must educate and enlighten people, beginning with your leaders. Then proceed one step at a time. Think in terms of years rather than weeks or even months. It can sometimes take years for Christians to mature in their areas of giftedness. The first stages are crucial.

'Love remains the most important ingredient in gift-centred ministry' (see 1 Cor. 13)